DISCARD

The Marriage Plan

The Marriage Plan

AGGIE JORDAN, PH.D.

HOW TO MARRY YOUR SOUL MATE

IN ONE YEAR OR LESS

Broadway Books New York

Broadway Books titles may be purchased for business or promotional use or for special sales. For information, please write to: Special Markets Department, Random House, Inc., 1540 Broadway, New York, NY 10036.

BROADWAY BOOKS and its logo, a letter B bisected on the diagonal, are trademarks of Broadway Books, a division of Random House, Inc.

Visit our website at www.broadwaybooks.com.

Library of Congress Cataloging-in-Publication Data

Jordan, Aggie, 1937–
The marriage plan: how to marry your soul mate in one year or less / Aggie Jordan.—1st ed.
p. cm.
Includes bibliographical references.
1. Mate selection. 2. Single women—Psychology. I. Title.
HQ801 .J68 2000
646.7'7—dc21
00-024887

FIRST EDITION

Designed by Dana Leigh Treglia

ISBN 0-7679-0601-2

00 01 02 03 04 10 9 8 7 6 5 4 3 2 1

Robert DeLaurenti, the love of my heart

and soul, and the six couples whose stories

are told in this book for their courage

and their support

Contents

CONTENTS

Preface

You want to get married because you hope it will bring you moments of great joy. You expect to have fun. You want to feel the warmth of his body as he envelops you, the soft touch of his hand to your face. You want to hear him whisper how beautiful you are. When love comes into your life, you know the excitement of being together, of being a part of his dreams and carried along to a life of mutual fulfillment.

I believe marriage was created for those who believe in themselves. It can be the ultimate happiness for those who have the confidence and courage to search for their soul mate. It's definitely not for the cowardly. It's for those who are hopeful, courageous, and ambitious. Happy marriages involve hard work and demand attention. The search itself also demands hard work and attention. Soul mates love each other deeply but they also must love themselves first. It takes courage and effort to work with the tension between this love of self and love of our mate.

I've taught goal setting to engineers, salespeople, secretaries, college professors, teachers, corporate instructors, military officers, forest rangers, and managers and executives in Fortune 500 companies. Goal setting is a technique that can help control both your personal life and business life. My story of setting and meeting a goal to get married in a short period of time, told in the chapter, "I Did It. So Can You" inspired people to set career goals, to set personal goals, and, yes, to set marriage goals.

The Marriage Plan: How to Marry Your Soul Mate in One Year— or Less was initially conceived by two friends, Cindy and Brenda, in a health spa in Michigan over twenty years ago. Over these years, with their support and the support of our mutual friend, Helen, I developed their initial concept into a workable strategy for my goal-setting classes and for this book. Thousands of women find themselves involved in relationships that are going nowhere; many others find themselves alone. Their souls search for their complements. *The Marriage Plan* describes how these women can meet and marry a life mate, a soul mate, within a short period of time.

If you wish to be in control of your life in a fulfilling marriage relationship, you can do it. You can follow this simple plan. I've done it. The six couples featured in this book did it. And our stories will help you to understand how we did it and why The Plan results in a happy marriage with a soul mate.

All of the couples who have gotten married according to *The Marriage Plan* have this in common: they didn't play games with their potential spouse. They wanted to build their marriage on a firm foundation, not on lies or mistrust or game playing. Many books on the market about male/female relationships, dating, and marriage advocate playing hard to get or deliberate deceit. These tactics will only lead to a marriage that's bound to be unhappy. A marriage built on this foundation will crumble.

I recorded the twelve interviews on tape and they were edited for easy reading. I've changed the names and locations to protect the couples' privacy. I chose these couples because I've been able to follow each couple from their meeting through most of their marriage. In addition to Cindy and Brenda and their husbands, I met the others in my goal-setting classes or through an international women's association.

If you want to get married but have been unable to find your mate, I hope that you'll recognize that you can succeed if you take control, set your goal, and do it. Come to this book with belief in yourself and with hope for thousands of joyful tomorrows. In places you'll find arrogance, because I believe strongly, even arrogantly, in the effectiveness of *The Marriage Plan*. You may be equally arrogant in your doubt. After all, you know hundreds of marriages that work without *The Marriage Plan*. Why should you take it seriously?

Because it works! If I irritate you with my unbending beliefs, don't stop reading. Be forgiving because it *will* work for you.

Believe that your soul mate is out there waiting for you and that marrying him can bring you ultimate happiness. Believe, too, that this book can help you find your soul mate and that happiness.

The Marriage Plan requires two personal strengths. You'll need the *desire* to get married and the *courage* to trust your own abilities to accomplish your goal. With *desire* and *courage* will come success!

A. J.

JUNE 2000

The Marriage Plan

Part One

MARRYING YOUR

SOUL MATE

WHAT IS A SOUL MATE?

Most people can get married if they want to by whatever deadline they set. They could be married in two weeks if they simply put an ad in the paper and take the first response. This, of course, is not what you want. You want to marry happily. You want someone to share your life and to grow in knowledge, wisdom, love, and joy. That's why *The Marriage Plan* is about marrying a *soul mate* not just getting a husband.

Many people ask me, "Can a person have more than one soul mate?" The answer, of course, is yes. Many people have experienced a soul mate's death and have found another. You may have a soul mate who is not someone you would want to marry. Perhaps you have a best friend whom you would call your soul mate.

We want to live in our spirit. Living in our own spirit means that we try to understand the depths of our being. Here is where our desires, our fantasies, our dreams, and our hopes live. These tell us what our soul is and wants, what motivates us, what makes us happy. Imagine that inside your soul are rooms of all kinds. Think of your soul as a castle to be explored, a rich array of talents and experiences that form your essence. Each of those rooms gleams with history, stories that make you who you are. Stories of sorrow are in one room, of pain in another, of mistakes in another, of guilt, of love, of achievement, of desires, of fulfillment, of nurturing, of friendships in others. Many rooms in that castle are yet to be filled. You would like your soul's complement to help you to fill them as you explore life.

Four important characteristics will help you to recognize your soul mate. The first is acceptance. He will accept you as you are. He does not try to change you. You want someone to listen to your dreams, to stimulate your mind, to understand your heart, to give you courage and confidence, and to give you love. You want someone to explore you physically, emotionally, and psychologically. You want someone to explore your mind, your ideas, your anger, and your joy. You want him to laugh with you and even cry with you.

He accepts your positive qualities (and you have plenty of them) and your negative ones (even the ones that irritate him). If there are too many of the latter then he is not your soul mate. Your soul mate recognizes that your strengths and weaknesses are like two sides of a coin. Both the negative and the positive characteristics make up who you are. You probably can't have one set without the other. It's part of being human.

Let's take an example. If you are assertive and maybe even aggressive, you probably get things accomplished in good measure and efficiently. A good thing! Perhaps you are also somewhat insensitive to other people because it simply takes too much time to consider their feelings. A not-so-good thing! Or let's imagine that you might be a nurturing, loving, giving person, but you also may tend to give to such an extent that you smother another with attention or even forget about your own needs. Often our strengths make us intolerant of others who don't have our strengths. The soul mate sees the balance and the beauty of both sides of you. He realizes if he tried to change you, he would also change those characteristics that attracted him to you in the first place. You too must remember the same about the person to whom you may become attracted. His strengths are also his weaknesses. If you can accept these, then he's your soul mate.

The second characteristic of a soul mate is generosity. The person with whom you are involved feels so much love for you that he is generous with his entire being. He first is generous with his time. This generosity means that he recognizes that not only does he want to be with you and talk to you but also he recognizes that relationships deepen only with personal contact. If one of you is out of town, you make arrangements to talk over the telephone, to e-mail, to communicate in whatever way you can. A soul mate is also generous with his energy. He's willing to devote his energy to learn about you, to participate in what you like to do, to give the energy to address your needs and to let you know his. Generosity also extends to financial caring. He's not stingy with his money. He's willing to share with you what he has. Even the person in dire straits can find ways to share. Generosity is not dependent on how much money one has.

All of these characteristics of generosity are also applicable to you. You too must be generous. If you find generosity does not characterize your relationship, then you are not soul mates. Someone once asked me if two selfish people can be soul mates. I suppose they can at the most primitive level but selfishness is not a long-term bond.

The third characteristic of a soul mate is that he is a learner. This means that your soul mate is constantly learning, as are you. Your soul mate must be curious about you, about what makes you tick, about your background, about your interests, your talents. He must want to learn about your personality and what makes you happy. He should also extend this curiosity to the outside world. The joys of marriage to a soul mate have to do with mutual exploration beyond the relationship. Although you both certainly won't have all the same interests in life, your ability to listen to each other and to get excited about the other's learning will excite and deepen the relationship.

My husband, Robert, is one of these great learners. We've been married for over twenty-five years and there is not a day I remember that he hasn't shared new knowledge. Now sometimes, I'm not the best listener when he goes into detail about topics that lose me, but I catch his excitement about some software advance, or a character in a book, or a new skiing technique, and it motivates me then to share what I've learned that day. It is this willingness to learn that will assure growth in a marriage and a permanent relationship.

The fourth characteristic is that a soul mate loves you madly. We'll talk more about falling and being in love later. A soul mate in or out of marriage appreciates who you are. This is much beyond the first characteristic of accepting your essence. This is a person who cares about your well-being, who thinks about your needs, and who is ready and able to support your choices.

Perhaps you've already been through one or more unhappy relationships. You know the circumstances of how you met, what brought you together. I'd wager that neither of you set a profile of the kind of person you wanted to marry. Or, if you did, it wasn't done with a thorough understanding of what would make a happy marriage for you. Did you look at marriage objectively? Rarely do we think about our deepest values after we fall in love. Objectivity has to come before we fall in love. If you're like most people, you experienced passion, or maybe just lust, tenderness, and fun. Someone cared for you and you for him. A security and comfort level met both your needs at the time.

Somehow that wasn't enough. The lust, the passion, the fun, the tenderness, the security, and the comfort dissipated. Perhaps there was love, not just *being* in love, but the love died. What was missing to keep it going? In most cases, the depth and caring that occurs between two soul mates was absent.

Television, movies, and commercials instill in us the importance of good looks, slim bodies, and a life without personal challenges. Those aren't values for a marriage of soul mates, a happy life partnership. A successful and happy life partnership unites two people who know what they want out of life and who agree that by sharing their lives they can achieve true happiness and satisfaction. Two people, who from the start of the relationship, become friends and communicate their deepest feelings, thoughts, and desires, will empower that relationship to grow. In exploring life they'll learn together about themselves and each other. When you find this friendship, this relationship, passion will be sparked and it will seal the bond. This communion that you've formed in friendship will feed your hunger.

In the process of working through *The Marriage Plan,* you'll take some time to learn what your soul needs. You'll try to be clear on what you want and send out signals during the year of your search only to those who look like soul mates. You won't waste time with unlikely candidates. Your soul mate will not play games with you, will accept you for who you are, and will respect your values. You'll know that your soul mate must have a great capacity to love you, a strong sense of integrity, and be open and willing to trust and to accept your trust.

Before getting to *The Plan* itself, let me tell you my own personal *Marriage Plan* success story and introduce you to the six couples who shared their relationships with me.

I DID IT, SO CAN YOU

Do you want to get married? Do you want roots? Do you want to stop the dating merry-go-round and find your soul mate? I did, and I worked at it with a number of men but without much success.

I had dated a man in Chicago quite seriously for three years when I took a job with General Motors Institute in Flint, Michigan, about three hundred miles away. Making a decision to leave someone I had been with for that long was difficult. When I met him, he was twenty-five, loved life, his Corvette T-top convertible, and, I hoped, me. A college development officer and a part-time law student, he was bright, well educated, and fun. I was thirty-three, a college dean, and looking for more depth to my life. I knew I wanted more than sex and fun. The relationship dissolved shortly after the move. Though I had learned much about myself and relationships, I discovered I had wasted three years of my life.

Most of my relationships began by falling in lust. A few went beyond that to limited intimacy and friendship. I wanted someone not only who would arouse my physical being but who would also awaken my desires to do and become my best. I wanted a soul mate, someone who would believe in my dreams, and I in his. Mutual respect for each other's talents and achievements would help us both to grow. I needed someone who would be generous with his time and energy and not see me as competition. My soul mate would respect who I was, like who I was, and wouldn't want to change me. I felt disillusioned that I would find this person.

I wasn't interested in sharing my life with a man who wanted to control or use me, or was insecure about who he was and what he wanted. With some men I felt like a sexy, exciting, loving woman capable of great sex and great love, and with others simply a ghost incarnate floating through my space and time, wondering if I'd ever find the man with whom I'd live forever.

I met Helen at my new job at GM. In direct contrast to me she demonstrated determination and openness about who she was and what she wanted.

"How long do you think it will take you to meet someone, fall in love, and marry," Helen asked me in her dining room on a Sunday afternoon as she pushed a pen and pad across the maple table. We had just cleaned up after an early Sunday dinner and her children had gone out to play with their friends. Her fiancé went fishing for the rest of the afternoon. She had decided the time had come for me to confront what I wanted out of life and she had a plan.

"By the time I'm forty," I answered jokingly.

"Four years from now is too long! Do *you* want to get married?"

The way she raised her inflection on the "you" compelled me to question momentarily what I thought I wanted. If I wanted to get married, why was I joking about it taking me four years?

"I *do* want to get married. You're right. Four years is too long."

Again she asked, "How long do you think it will take you to meet a man, fall in love, and marry him?"

Helen's voice was intimidating. She was demanding an answer, boring a hole into me, opening me up so that I could see what I was doing to myself.

"If you want to get married in two weeks, you can do it. You can put an ad in the paper and you'll have plenty of possibilities." She said this only partly in jest.

Where was she going with this? I thought. "That's crazy, Helen, I'm not going to marry a man from an ad."

"At least it wouldn't take four years. People do get married from ads in the paper," she said.

"I'm not going to do that. I'm a reasonable person."

"Okay, then how long will it take you, Miss Reasonable? Evidently somewhere between two weeks and four years."

"A year," I mumbled. A year seemed reasonable.

"What did you say? Say it out loud."

"A year," I raised my volume some.

"Let's go. Let's start working on that year. So one year from today, January twelfth." It was cold and dreary outside, not a time of year I'd pick for a wedding.

"I'll do it by December. I'll be married before my thirty-seventh birthday." I had set my goal. But Helen wouldn't be satisfied.

"Write that down."

I wrote the words, "I want to get married by December seventh." My stomach started to tighten. Did I mean it? I did want to get married and I knew I had to admit it and mean it. The moment I suggested the date, I was committed.

"What kind of man do you want to marry?" Helen asked, probing again. "If you want just any man, I assure you the ad in the paper will get you married within two weeks."

"I don't want to be married so much that I'll accept *any* man. I want a man that I can share my life with, and that man has to accept me as I am. That's important to me. I'll always have a career. I don't know if I want children. I think I don't. And I'm independent. I'm not going to be anybody's slave. We'll have to be partners."

"Fine, that's step number one: Find a man who will accept you as you. Write it down."

I wrote on the pad: "I want a partner to accept me as I am."

"Why do you want to get married? If you're so independent, maybe it's best if you stay single."

"I'd like to find someone who's self-reliant, has his own set of interests, is intelligent, and has a good job. I'm not going to support him. I want him to be independent too."

"Write it down."

I did what I was told.

"What about age? Do you have any preference? Younger? Older? By how much?"

"I want someone around my age. I'd like him to be between the ages of thirty-five and forty-five. Maybe a little older, certainly not too much younger." I saw the age difference with the man I'd dated for three years as the reason the relationship failed. It was more a matter of maturity than age but I didn't want to make that mistake again.

"What about physical features?"

"He doesn't have to be a Greek god. Some hunks are so ego-tistical I couldn't live with them."

"Write it down," she said.

"Does he have to have money?"

"I can make my own money and I'm willing to share it but wealth isn't that important to me. Actually I think I'd prefer that he wouldn't have it. I'd hate to be indebted to someone. I'd rather we both worked at building our future together."

"Write that down," she said again. I did.

"What about his education? You have a Ph.D. Does he have to be that educated?"

"No. He definitely doesn't have to have a Ph.D. I've dated my share of those and I prefer not to have that kind of competition in my marriage. I'm sure that I can find one who won't see me as competition but I'd rather not zero in on that population. I would like him to have a degree or at least an area of interest that he's pursued. The most important thing is for him to be interesting. He's got to have his own interests."

"Are there any other characteristics?"

"He's got to be able to communicate. I'm not going to be stuck with someone who keeps everything in. I want someone who will express himself. He'll have to be direct and not play games with me. He's definitely got to be trustworthy and honest. Integrity is very important to me."

This time I voluntarily began to write: "Good communicator and honest."

"What is something you absolutely can't live with?"

"You mean different from those things I've already written down?"

"Yes."

"There's one other very important characteristic to me. You're not going to like this but he can't be divorced and I don't want someone with kids."

Helen had three children and had been married twice. I didn't want her to take this personally but I was quite serious. We moved on into the living room to get comfortable for the rest of this discussion.

"Why not? Why don't you want to marry a divorced man?" she questioned as she sat opposite me in the large brown-and-white print chair.

"I don't want to have problems with a second family. I don't want to be someone's stepmother." A voice in my head appeared saying, Catholic girls don't marry divorced men.

With her head on her hands, Helen bore her big, dark eyes into me and summed up our talk:

"Look at the profile you just drew. He'll accept you as you are, is secure in his own ego, fairly intelligent, self-reliant, independent, and between the ages of thirty-five and forty-five. Now tell me, what percentage of the population do you think you're going to find with those characteristics who has never been married? I'd say that you've just made your goal nearly impossible. The men who have never been married are not necessarily any better than divorced men. They probably have more problems."

"Wait a minute. Just because I'm single at my age doesn't mean I have problems."

"Exactly my point. You're passing judgment on divorced people, aren't you?"

She made some sense but I was adamant. No divorced man for me. Helen, convinced that she couldn't make me see reason, went on.

"What steps are you going to take to find this man? Where will you meet him?"

Unlike a few women I knew who had met their husbands in a bar, the bars wouldn't work for me. The only other alternatives I could think of were church, work, and friends. Since I had been a weekly attendant at church and hadn't met anyone, what were the chances that I would? I chose instead the most logical places for me.

"Work! Friends! Perhaps I could join a club or a volunteer organization working for a charity."

"That's a good place to start. How will you get your friends and people at work to introduce you to some prospects?"

I knew what was coming. Helen and I were project managers in the Management Education Division at General Motors Institute. Among the management courses we taught to managers from all over General Motors was goal setting. I recognized what I had to do but I was silent.

"Who are you going to tell?"

The question was painful. Single women, especially ones who are thirty-six-years old and without any male in the picture, don't want to simply announce to friends and coworkers that they have a plan to get married.

"Who will help you?"

"You. Won't you?"

"I don't count. Let's list the people who will help you."

This time I didn't voluntarily pick up the pen. I began to see myself telling some of the people at work: "I want to get married."

Hell, they would laugh at me. "This is stupid. I can't do that. Can't you see my saying that to Tom [my boss]? He'll think I've lost a screw."

"Well, you don't have to tell Tom. Who do you think will take you seriously?"

"Probably Roger."

I started a list of some friends with whom I felt I could share this goal, as uncomfortable as it might be, and who would be willing to help me. It was short. At the top, of course, was Helen. Next came Roger, a friend and coworker with whom I had been team-teaching some classes. Next came my dear friend Marg, who was an assistant professor at Michigan State University. She had just been recently married. I knew both she and her husband would help. That made four people I could count on to help me with this goal. I began to feel slightly more confident.

"Marg and I have discussed my wanting to get married," I said. "This is different. Now that I've a plan, a goal, even a date, and a list of characteristics that I want in a man, it seems so calculating. Where is my knight in shining armor? I'm not supposed to be out there searching. He's supposed to be pursuing, wooing me. Admitting to anybody else that I have this plan will surely make me look desperate. I'm not desperate and I don't want them to think I am."

"You already made that clear to me," Helen said. "If you were desperate, you'd have taken any man. You didn't and you won't. Why shouldn't you be in control of getting married? Why should we, supposedly sophisticated women, wait until 'the right man' comes around?"

The sun was starting to go down and Helen rose, saying, "Let's have a drink." As she was preparing my Johnnie Walker

Red and her old-fashioned she said, "You set goals to get your degree. You even set goals to go to Europe, to buy furniture, to advance in your career. Why wouldn't you have a plan for the most important decision of your life, finding a man who could be your life mate? You've made up your mind that you want to get married and now you have to send out the signal to your soul mate. You have to be very clear with the people on this list and with the men you date. Who will you tell tomorrow?"

The process of goal setting demands that there be an immediate action step. One must do something "tomorrow." You can't wait until next week or next month. My stomach pulled ever tighter at the word "tomorrow."

Since I had been teaching with Roger, I decided he'd be the first person I'd tell. He was married and I thought he was someone who would take me seriously. I didn't want to be the laughing-stock of General Motors.

I understood goal setting and I knew it worked in management and in other areas of my life that I control. I couldn't control another person that I didn't even know. But that wasn't the point. I could control myself. Now all I needed was confidence, trust in myself, and perseverance.

"Don't give up," Helen said. "You've already taken the hardest step. Remember, others may laugh at you, may even think you're desperate, but you know you're not. You're in control. Now get the message out."

That night I stewed over the commitment I had made not just to Helen but to myself. The next morning the first person I saw was Roger. More than serendipity, it was a confirmation that I was on the right track. I invited Roger for coffee. As we sat and sipped I was determined I was going to tell him but I seemed speechless. Finally I said, "Roger, I want to get married." No preface, no information about how Helen and I had worked on goal setting, just "I want to get married."

As I had feared but not expected, Roger said, "That's great, Ag. Wait six months, I'll divorce Barbara and marry you." Of course he was jesting, but feeling as vulnerable as I did, I felt hurt. I became angry that he wouldn't take me seriously and I said, my head bending toward his, "Roger, I'm serious." I explained to him what Helen and I did the night before and then said, "I want to get married, and I want to meet someone, and I want you to help me do that."

He finally took me seriously and in his caring way responded, "Aggie, I'll help you. I'm not sure I know anybody good enough for you but with all the single men who we meet here at GMI, we'll find some possibilities."

By the end of the day everyone at work knew that I wanted to get married. Roger hadn't told them. I did. I had coworkers dropping by and telling me that they had cousins and friends to whom they would like to introduce me. It seemed to be working but weeks went by and a I found that they weren't as serious about it as I was. My directness was probably not acceptable to them. Women just don't do that. We are supposed to wait and wait and *wait* for the right man to come along. I became frustrated but Helen kept encouraging me. Many times she introduced me to people in her classes that she thought were eligible but nothing clicked.

The spring came and three months had passed with no sign of any potential mate. During this year, 1974, General Motors was meeting its first energy crisis. It had never laid anyone off. We used to say of General Motors, "No one is fired, we only retire." It was a shock to me when I was called in to my boss and told that

I'd be laid off in two weeks. I had given up an excellent job as a dean at a university to come to GMI but as the last one hired I was the first one to go. It did not make me happy. Ten months earlier they had hired ten minorities and females to fulfill an affirmative action goal and they laid us all off in one fell swoop. Helen was lucky. She had two years of seniority on us and kept her job.

I now had to readjust my energy. I was desperate, not for a man, but for a job. Knowing my state of mind, Helen wouldn't let me lose sight of my goal: "You've met a bump in the road but you can't change that goal. Perhaps this is God's way of telling you that the person you're going to marry isn't here." I was a strong believer in Divine Providence but the turn of events was so surprising that I wasn't able to balance my thinking. Thankfully, Helen's words reminded me this world isn't entirely under my control.

Getting a job wasn't easy. Most companies were suffering with the energy crisis. All of Michigan was touched by it. I wanted to stay in Michigan but I was having no luck.

A friend and former colleague, Barry, had moved to Martin Marietta Aerospace Company in Orlando, Florida, earlier in the year. He called to ask me to interview for an opening he had. I told him that I wanted to stay in Michigan.

"Why?" he asked.

"Because I want to get married."

"Have you met anyone?"

"No."

"You know you can meet someone in Florida as well as in Michigan," he said, a grin in his voice.

I told him I'd think about it. He called back within a week with an unusual offer. He raised the salary and added:

"My boss said to tell you that we did a study here in Orlando and there are two thousand bachelors between the ages of thirty-five and fifty. It's the bachelor capital of the world. We'll help you find someone."

My social life in Orlando was generally barren and I wasn't crazy about the defense industry. Barry and others did keep their word to me but I had no interest in the men they introduced.

I had been working in Orlando six weeks when Ed, an acquaintance whose desk was near the coffee vending machines, called to me as I dropped my change into the machine for coffee.

"Aggie, come here, I want you to meet a friend, Robert DeLaurenti."

I looked at Robert and he was very good-looking. He looked within the age range and evidently had a job. I wonder if he's a prospect, I thought. I looked down at his left hand. He had a class ring where there could've been a wedding ring. My hopes rose. All this in thirty seconds at the coffee machines. We had a brief conversation and I went back to my office.

The phone rang. "I met you this morning. I'd love to take you to dinner and get to know you better." My heart began to flutter. This was a real date for dinner, not "Let's go for coffee," or "Come up and see my etchings." For a brief moment I wondered if I should play hard to get but my instinct took over and I realized that this was a good first step toward meeting a man who met my profile. We settled on a time. I began to strengthen my faith in Divine Providence (and in goal setting).

I proceeded to Barry's office to tell him and also to see if he knew Robert. He didn't know him, but we did have access to personnel records. We were, after all, in human resources. Being a strong supporter of mine, and looking out for my best interests, he got one of our colleagues, Carol, to bring up Robert's record.

"Aggie, you can't go out with him," Barry said as we stood over the microfiche. "He's married with four children."

My heart fell. The woman who wouldn't even date a divorced man had accepted an invitation from a married man.

Carol was more reasonable. "Wait a minute. The man asked you out for dinner. He didn't ask you to marry him. Why don't you go out, have a nice dinner, find out if he's still married? If he is, tell him you don't date married men. If he isn't, then take it from there."

The evening came for our date. When he rang the doorbell, I prayed: Oh, please, don't let him be married. If he was divorced, I'd have actually felt lucky.

Within five minutes I learned that the personnel records were badly outdated. He had been divorced for two years and had been living in Orlando with two of his four children. He was slightly late for our date because he had to be sure that the girls had their dinner and were settled for the evening.

We went to dinner and dancing afterward. I felt so right as we danced. We flowed to the music in each other's arms. We fit so well. He then asked me out the next evening and the next evening. I learned that my rule about divorced men with children was based on theory. This man was *real*. Was I willing to give up this wonderful man just because he was divorced?

The following week his ex-wife was coming into town and I wouldn't be able to see him. He told me he'd call me on Saturday and he'd like us to make plans for Saturday night. In the meantime I called Helen, who knew from my voice that I'd been badly smitten.

"Did you tell him?"

Goal setting requires that you tell the person who can most help you meet your goal. Before I got too emotionally involved I had to tell Robert that my goal was to get married. I had only been out with him three times and I certainly wasn't ready to tell him yet. Helen persisted. She knew that I'd be wasting time if he and I weren't on the same wavelength about marriage.

"You must tell him, Aggie, the next time you see him. I don't want you to waste time or get hurt. I can hear it in your voice. You're starting to get hooked."

After Robert and I returned to my house on Saturday night we talked for hours as we did on all of our dates. We didn't have sex although we hugged and kissed. There was still a lot we didn't know about each other. I was torn about telling him. But I had to.

"Robert, we've gone out four times now."

I almost choked on my words. How was I going to say this?

"I want you to know that I'm starting to fall in love with you and I don't want to get hurt. I've a goal to get married and I don't want to waste time with our relationship if that's not where you are."

"Is this an ultimatum?" he asked.

"No, it's not an ultimatum. It is, however, a statement about where I want to be headed."

"I'm falling in love with you too, Aggie. I do want to marry again and I'd like to work on it with you."

Working at getting married is the beginning of the commitment. It isn't the same as saying, "I want to marry you." What Robert was saying was that he wanted us to get to know each other better. He wanted our relationship to develop. It also meant that our relationship was to be exclusive. It had to be if it was going to develop into a lifetime marriage.

———

During the next five weeks, we learned quite a bit about each other. He was Catholic, forty years of age, had a good position in aerospace procurement, and had a great sense of humor. We shared core values of honesty and integrity. We discussed finances, sex, children, careers, and our future together. He talked about his thirteen years of marriage, from the development of that relationship to its dissolution. He was frank about problems in his marriage and how we might avoid the same.

We talked about his children. The oldest girl, Mary, was his ex-wife's daughter and Robert had helped raise her since she was two. Mary made the choice to live with Robert at the time of the divorce. To me, this spoke volumes about his character. As I heard each story in his life and about his children, I fell more deeply in love with him.

Two weeks after our commitment conversation Robert proposed and I accepted. Although we were both confident of our sexual compatibility, it was now time for assurance. When we made love, it was everything we had hoped.

On October fourth we were married, seven weeks after our first date and two months ahead of my schedule.

We're still happily married and our children have grown up quite nicely. We like to take some credit for that. It wasn't easy for them or for me all of the time. But it's not easy for biological parents either. We made it through and we have a deep love and respect for each other. I'm so glad that I adjusted my goal and discovered that divorced men and their children can bring great joy.

What follows is Robert's story. He'll tell you how he believes that setting a goal works from his perspective.

Robert's Story

I had been married for thirteen years, divorced for two. I set a goal to get married again. I felt more comfortable married, if I could find someone I could love and someone who could love me. I didn't want to date women who didn't want to get married. At my age it was pointless.

I wanted to make sure that the woman I dated was one that I could get along and have fun with. She had to be smart and someone I could talk to, to solve problems with. She didn't have to be book smart so much as smart in the ways of life. I think people who let their emotions run their lives are not using their brains to solve their problems.

More important than all other criteria was that I marry someone who was capable of loving and understanding me. I also wanted someone who was working, so we could build financial security together. Both my mother and father worked together for years. They owned a bakery. My mother had a hand and say in just about everything that happened in the home and in the bakery. I lived with that feeling growing up and I wanted that in marriage.

Unmarried with four children, two of whom lived with me and two with their mother three thousand miles away, I had a difficult time and it took me a long time to start dating again. I was dating a little but there was no one whom I even thought about marrying.

You know how I met Aggie. What you don't know is that I was quite taken with her at that coffee vending machine. Although it was hard for me to ask women out, I didn't hesitate this time. I picked up that phone and some-how knew she'd say yes.

She's a warm person and we enjoyed being together. We'd stay up until three or four in the morning talking about everything. I fell in love with her almost immedi-ately, certainly by the second date. I knew we'd be happy together. It was a close, easy, and comfortable relationship. The chemistry was there.

After I dated Aggie for a week, my ex-wife came down to visit me. It had been planned for some time. We were going to see if we could get back together. I didn't think we could but was willing to try. It just absolutely didn't work out. I no longer loved her and I wasn't com-fortable with her. I tried for the kids' sake. They were very unhappy about being split apart. I was brought up to be-lieve that marriage was forever but this wasn't going to work.

After this I knew I wanted to date Aggie. I was very comfortable with her and I wanted to do things to make her happy. My days were long and my nights were short. I wanted to be with her all the time but we had to work!

Men often talk about many things with other men, sports cars, and politics but rarely the intimacy of personal feelings or problems. Women have an easier time talking about the things that are important. I could talk about everything with Aggie. There was an intimacy that wasn't there with other women.

We went out with the children a lot in those seven weeks. Aggie was very attentive to the children, probably more than I was. It was important to me that both she and the children be happy. If they didn't get along, the marriage wouldn't work.

We took a Saturday trip to the ocean with Gina, my second daughter. For the entire forty-five-minute drive, Gina talked to Aggie about *Jeremiah Johnson*, a movie she had seen the night before. Gina was only thirteen but Aggie would ask her questions and would listen to what she had to say. That was really important to me.

We talked about getting married almost from the beginning. I decided I'd invite my two daughters, Gina and Mary, to dinner when I proposed to Aggie. I wanted the girls to be a part of the whole thing. Aggie and I had talked about it so often that I didn't think she'd say no to my proposal; she might say maybe. I decided my chances were good enough to take the risk of having the children there. Our commitment was sealed when I proposed and she accepted and I gave her a ring. We knew it was right.

In spite of the short time we knew each other, I was sure that Aggie loved me and had the capability to grow in that love. It was the way she spoke to the children, and the seriousness and openness with which we talked. She was straightforward and she never tried to manipulate me or play games with me. I tried not to do so with her. We were honest and direct, even though sometimes it hurt. This was an intimacy and feeling that I never experienced before.

Aggie founded Jordan-DeLaurenti, Inc., a training company, and I worked with her to set it up. I helped with the bookkeeping and whatever else she needed to make it successful. After five years, I joined the company full-time and worked for her. Although this might be a problem for many men, it was never a problem for me because Aggie and I share the same values. We have a mutual respect for one another, integrity between us and with our employees, fidelity in marriage and loyalty to each other within the business.

My life has been happy with Aggie. I believe that when you know what you're about, when you set goals and are determined to reach them, you send out a very special message. It isn't only in the way you speak but also in the way you look and the way you carry yourself. The energy is there. Others do pick it up and act on it. When your goal is to get married, those who have the same goal will pick up your signals. When you get together with someone of the same interest and find mutual love, something great will happen.

From Robert's testimony I hope you can see that our marriage is one of soul mates and our meeting was truly fateful. I set the goal in January, was laid off in April, moved to Florida in July, met Robert in August, and we were married in October.

In the next chapter you will learn about the couples we interviewed about their soul mate marriages. I have drawn a profile of them so that you will know a little about each before they let you into their lives in the remaining chapters.

OTHERS DID IT TOO:
THE COUPLES' STORIES

The couples interviewed for this book and whose stories I tell represent a diversity of ethnic cultures, religions, education levels, ages, numbers of past marriages, and careers. There are two African-American couples, several first-generation Americans, a Jew, several Catholics, some Protestant denominations, and some with no religious affiliation. There's a variety of undergraduate and master's degrees as well as a high school nongraduate. We have a real estate agent, several entrepreneurs, an attorney, two construction contractors, several corporate executives and managers, a politician, a nurse, an engineer, and the head of a nonprofit agency. Three in the group are recovering alcoholics. Several finally found love and happiness after three marriages; two are in their first marriage; and seven are in their second marriages. The length of the couples' marriages ranges from two to twenty-six years.

Even with all these differences in marital, cultural, educational, and business backgrounds, few differences exist in the expectations each woman had for finding her soul mate. They all chose a partner whom they could love and respect and who would love and respect them. They married within their race and generally shared a spiritual belief system but not necessarily a religion.

They share four common characteristics:

- In all six marriages one of the mates set a goal to get married.
- They all value their marriages and state in one way or another that they're happy with their spouses.
- They're all hardworking people who have struggled for and attained financial stability.
- They all have had the experience of children, whether they're their biological or adopted children or stepchildren.

Background on the Couples

JESSIE AND PAUL

Paul and Jessie are a high-powered couple. I met Jessie at some management and goal-setting seminars that I did for her company. Twenty-nine, petite, with short salt-and-pepper hair, she was an up-and-coming executive who was in the process of a divorce. Jessie is bright, caring, ambitious, and capable. Today she's the president of a large and prestigious division of a Fortune 500 company. She was and still is a strong feminist leader. Although she's been at the top in corporate America, she hasn't hesitated to take a stand for women.

She has a great instinct for corporate politics and understands her business. Along with her drive for corporate success, she felt a strong need for a successful love and marriage relationship, despite a failed first marriage.

Paul, tall and athletic, with sandy blond hair and a smile that warms everyone he meets, came into Jessie's life shortly after her divorce. He was a twenty-eight-year-old bachelor attorney who loved to sail, play trombone, and enjoy life.

After three long-term relationships, he set criteria for the woman he was going to marry. He wanted a partnership where both could be independent yet share core values, intimacy, and friendship.

Jessie and Paul, who are loving parents, encountered difficulties as a two-career couple with children. Jessie, like many women, is the glue that holds the family circle together while Paul learned how to become a contributing father and a more understanding husband. Their struggle is not over, because their children are young. They seem, however, to have deepened their relationship.

LAURA AND STAN

Laura also worked for a Fortune 500 company and attended one of my seminars on goal setting. A tall strawberry blonde with hair that fell to her shoulders and a pink complexion, she married her first husband, Vince, when she was still a teenager. For the last ten years of the marriage, Vince was a self-destructive alcoholic. Although she cared for him she finally divorced him because living with him was so painful.

Stan, a coworker and friend of Laura's, was in his late forties and divorced. Both set criteria for a future mate, whom they weren't sure they would ever find. Even though they both knew they didn't want to be alone, they couldn't bring themselves to say, "I want to get married." They mistrusted their own ability to make a second marriage successful.

Stan and Laura were always attracted to each other, although not necessarily sexually, in their work relationship. They have complementary but very different personalities. He's calm and reserved and she's more energetic and outgoing. Their friendship makes it work. Each of them is in control of his or her own life, which makes both of them in control of their marriage.

SUSAN AND MARK

Susan, a successful manager in another Fortune 500 company, wasn't only an attendee in our management seminars but was a fully trained leader. Thin and five foot seven, with an engaging laugh and a sense of humor that makes her exceptionally likable, it wasn't difficult for her to attract men. Mark, a dark Italian who was a little taller and somewhat older than twenty-five-year-old Susan, had a bright future as an engineering manager at the same company. He had been previously married and had two young sons. Susan, energetic about love but not naive, was disillusioned by her experiences with the men she had dated. She had decided that perhaps marriage was never going to be for her—until she met Mark.

This is the only story that is told from one side. Recently Mark suffered a stroke and communicates with great difficulty. Susan, his interpreter, loves him deeply. Despite all the pain and illness, she still considers Mark her support, her best friend, and her soul mate. She feels totally blessed to have Mark in her life.

Thomas Moore believes that the mystery of love involves fate. He says: "When fate throws us into confusion, people must talk from the heart so as to meet life exactly at it presents itself" (*Soul Mates,* HarperCollins, 1994). Susan and Mark, denied their normal communication, talk to each other from the heart.

CINDY AND CLIFF

Cindy, a dynamic woman of five four who has exercised for an hour a day every day for the last thirty years, has been my support, my rock, and my good friend for many of those years. I've watched her cope with both the joys and the vicissitudes of life: setting a goal to get married; being engaged to Jim; meeting and marrying Cliff; and struggling, along with me, to raise our teenagers. She rose to the position of director of human resources for the corporate offices of one of the largest corporations in America, became the vice president of a large medical information company, and recently formed her own construction development company with Cliff. In Cindy, you'll see the growth of a woman who has found her soul mate after two failed marriages and a love affair.

Cliff and Cindy are an African-American couple who have raised nine children between them. Cliff, six years her junior, also had two painful, failed marriages, and being alone brought him peace. He liked it that way. He has a sense of humor, many times at his own expense. Humor wasn't always his saving grace. Sometimes the stress of developing a mason contracting business intensified and he found solace in alcohol and, as he said, "It started to get out of hand."

Cliff fell in love with Cindy on their first date. This is not the case with all of our couples, most of whom developed deep friendships before they fell in love. Cliff and Cindy's intimacy and Cindy's determination to execute her plan gave them a foundation for a very exciting, fulfilling, successful marriage.

BRENDA AND JOHNNY

Johnny and Brenda are also African American. Johnny is Brenda's third husband. Always a strong woman both physically and mentally, Brenda allowed two failed marriages to emotionally paralyze her for several years. Before her second marriage she set a goal to get married with inadequate criteria. The wrong criteria for your mate can doom a marriage. Her spirituality and the strong self-image that her parents gave her finally opened her up to Johnny. Her pain and suffering was great. Her happiness today is even greater. She's a successful elected politician, the president of a nonprofit corporation, and a person who found her soul mate in Johnny.

For most of his adulthood Johnny's life was in the gutter. Irresponsible, a manipulator of people and systems, Johnny was a "miserable father." After twenty-two tries in treatment centers, he was still an unfulfilled, miserable human being. After his final recovery he met Brenda.

Johnny set criteria for the kind of relationship he wanted. He also set goals for the kind of communication and interaction he wanted to have with his soul mate when he found her. Johnny is very direct and open. He did not play games in their courtship nor does he in marriage. He talks about adding a little "yeast" to stories to make them interesting but that's the extent of his trifling with honesty.

Honesty can be difficult between two people. Brenda did not always appreciate it. And although Johnny and Brenda are in love after fifteen years of marriage, it wasn't always that way. However, they always respected and trusted one another and their love has deepened over the years. They give each other space while sharing many common interests. Their intimacy is based on trust and a truly open pattern of communication.

AIMÉE AND DON

I interviewed Aimée and Don thirteen months after their marriage. They were married one year from the day that Aimée had set as her wedding date. When Aimée set her goal, she had only been out with Don once and she hadn't looked upon him as a potential mate.

Aimée, a tall, striking redhead and successful entrepreneur, had two long-term relationships in addition to her first marriage in which her children were born. She did not want for dates but realized over the years that the men with whom she developed a relationship were narcissistic and incapable of loving anyone. In setting her criteria, she wanted someone less selfish and more loving.

Don, a real estate broker and a lover of horses, had also set a goal to get married. He had learned a great deal about himself in the years before his marriage to Aimée, especially from belonging to a men's support group which had a great influence on his re-thinking the process of selecting female companions. He discovered that the women to whom he was physically and sexually attracted were women with childhood wounds. The relationships were disastrous. He felt naively that he could heal these women and that they in turn would heal him. He knew he had to meet a different kind of woman and get to know her as a friend before he started forming a relationship.

During a period of two years Don took more than one hundred women to lunch before he met Aimée. Lunch gave him a safe environment to get to know a woman before dating her. It was Aimée, however, who set the tone for their relationship. She wasn't going to continue dating someone who wasn't interested in marriage. Don and Aimée were both in control of the kind of person they were going to marry and the terms under which they dated. This control and honesty with themselves and each other laid the foundation for their happiness.

In the pages that follow, the couples allow you an intimate view of their lives, including their courtships and their marriages. They share with us what it takes to make a marriage work even when you marry your soul mate.

Each chapter in Part Two introduces a step of The Plan. The next chapter, for example, discusses the importance of setting your goal. You'll learn why it is important to set a goal and that you should have no fear that someone might think you're desperate if you do. You'll learn that giving up the Cinderella myth will help you to be objective. You'll learn how you keep true to who you are, to your essence, and that if you want to get married you need to discover if what you're doing matches your goal. Setting the goal with a time deadline is the first step, and it gives you the power to control your future.

Part Two

The Steps
of the Plan

STEP ONE: SET YOUR GOAL

Do You Want to Get Married?

If you bought this book, undoubtedly you are considering that marriage would make you happy. Marriage is a choice we make. Not everyone makes that choice, but for those who do, it is a choice to be happy with another. If you are going to make that choice, you'll want to be sure that it's right for you. You'll ask yourself why and what will it do for you as opposed to being single. You won't want fear to obstruct your answer.

People who think about marriage are often fearful that if they admit they want to get married, they may not find someone. They see so many people divorced that they are afraid they'll make a mistake. They are sometimes afraid of love and intimacy, of being hurt by both. They often look at the negatives instead of the positives. As you approach the task of setting a goal to get married, be in touch with your soul, your internal spirit, your instincts. When you feel fear, challenge it. Don't give in to it but dig into the core of that fear and know that the two master motivators of all of us are love and fear. If fear is in control, love is not.

Besides fear, many other things can affect our ability to make choices, such as conflicting desires, a lack of focus, or an uninformed perspective. We can determine what we want and go after it, if we examine why we do what we do. Getting married is about love. Is the desire for the love of a soul mate motivating you? This chapter will help you to determine if it is, so be courageous and act.

Why Do You Want
to Get Married?

People want to get married for many reasons. Some because they want to have children. Others because they fall in lust or even in love and believe they want to spend the rest of their life with the object of their attraction. Some because they're afraid of growing old alone. People choose to get married at different stages of their lives. Through the centuries women particularly had a mate chosen for them at an early age. In the first three-quarters of this century most people chose their mates for love but they got married in their late teens or early twenties because it was expected of them. They may not have been mature enough to have married their soul mate at that early age.

Why have over half the marriages of the fifties and sixties in the United States ended in divorce? Many sociologists, psychologists, and economists have hypothesized that this is due to the liberalism of the sixties, the sexual revolution, women's liberation, the drug culture, the "I" generation, and many other sociological phenomena. Whatever the reasons for the dissolution of so many marriages, the statistic should not frighten us.

The people in this book had a variety of reasons for getting married. I wanted to get married because I wanted roots. I wanted to belong to someone. I wanted the companionship of a mate. My husband, Robert, wanted to get married because he thought he'd be happier married than unmarried. Aimée, Brenda, and Cindy wanted to get married because they were unhappy in their single state. They were tired of forming relationships, investing time and energy in them, and then having them fall apart. Don wanted to get married because he wanted a soul mate, one who would support him in his life journey and one he could support in her life goals. Paul wanted to get married because he always viewed himself as a husband and father. Others had such bad marriages, such pain and suffering, that they didn't want to get married again. They changed their minds when their soul mate came into their lives.

It's time for you now to decide why you want to be married. Complete this sentence:

I want to get married because _____

_____.

If You Want to Get Married,

What Are You Doing?

Do you believe that you can find a soul mate, a life partner? Do you believe that you can fall in love and marry him within a reasonable time? Do you believe this even when there's no man in your life at this moment? You can have a happy, fulfilling marriage if you have the desire and the commitment. But you must want it badly enough.

Often we would like to believe that life's circumstances have been chosen for us. We blame others or outside events for the paths we've chosen. But we've chosen the path if we take action; we're responsible for our choices. No matter what pressures we face, we make the choices.

I often hear people say they want to go back to school and get a degree. Or I hear people say they want to leave their job and start their own business. Or that they want to build their dream house. Yet too often they make no effort toward that goal and instead find meaningless excuses to do something else. I hear other people say they would like to meet someone and marry, yet they don't work toward fulfilling that want. Not until we act do we get what we want. Our behavior tells us what we want in this life. What we want may be no fear, no risk, no challenge, no deep friendship, and no soul mate. Are we acting as though we're afraid of risk? If so, we need to face this fear. We need to understand that it's depriving us of a joyous, fulfilling life.

Why do we remain in bad situations? A dysfunctional marriage? A negative relationship? A self-destructive job situation?

We see the damage they do, yet we continue. We have the knowledge to take positive action but we don't act.

A dear friend of mine, Sheila, was in a psychologically abusive marriage for years. She's bright, well educated, respected in her field of chemical engineering, but slow to recognize her own needs versus those of others in her family, her husband and her son. I listened patiently to her complain many times.

Her husband, a professor, was having an affair with a young student. He continued to tell my friend that he wasn't sleeping with the student but simply shared an apartment with her and two other students, fifty miles away from home, because it was more conveniently located near the university and saved money in commuting. She believed him. Finally I told her I thought she wanted to live with that abuse, or she'd do something about it. Eventually she left him when she learned that nobody was keeping her in that situation but herself and her fears of the unknown. He later married the student twenty-five years his junior and had a child with her. Sheila has not yet found the love of her life because she's again settled for living with a man who doesn't abuse her but doesn't add much to her life either except that she's not alone.

You may argue that we stay in dysfunctional situations not because we want to but because we're afraid, or our financial condition won't allow it, or it's best for the children, or a thousand other reasons. Do we love ourselves so little that we think all others are more important than our own well-being? Are my children truly better off when I'm allowing myself to be abused? Don't I think enough of myself to risk finding a new job when I know the one I have is beating me down? Don't I trust myself enough to believe that I'm worthy of doing better? Is it lack of courage or lack of will that keeps me from taking positive steps for my own life? The bottom line is we do what we do because we want to, because we refuse to do otherwise. Our messages to ourselves keep us captive. To be free to control our own lives, we must send ourselves liberating messages.

Thomas Moore, whose two books *Care of the Soul* and *Soul Mates* were on the *New York Times* bestseller list for months, tells us that we know the answers to our conflicts in life. The answers are in our soul. By soul, he means the life spirit within us, the energy that makes us sound and whole and in tune with our reason for existence. Fantasy and imagination are the messages of the soul. We'll know what we want if we listen to our fantasies, our daydreams, and our imagination. If our soul longs for a mate, if we want a life companion who will respect us for who we are, we can have it. We can have what we want, if we listen to our soul and act on what it tells us.

You're Not Desperate

A young, unmarried friend with whom I was discussing *The Marriage Plan* told me, "I'm going to buy the book because I want to read it but I won't put it on my coffee table! People will think I'm desperate." Why do women think that it's humiliating to want to get married? It's not! The majority of humans marry. Everyone is hoping to find a soul mate. We want a man who loves and respects us for who we are. We don't want him to change us. We all want to be appreciated for our great personalities, our keen minds, our accomplishments, our splendid bodies, but most of all for the love we can give and the love we want to receive. So why are we afraid to admit this to our family and friends?

Setting a goal to get married doesn't mean we're desperate to find a man. Getting married to the wrong person is far worse than being alone. The search for a life partner is so special to us we want to preserve it from the jesters of the world. We don't want others to make fun of us, to ridicule us because we haven't found the right man. There's a sacredness about the meaning of a life partner. After all, we do expect him to be one with us, to live in the same home, to be happy in our company, and (for some of us) to have and raise children with us. These are sacred desires because they touch the core of who we are and who we'll become.

It doesn't mean you're desperate if you want this. You know what you want and you won't settle for less. If you were desperate, you could find a man in less than two weeks. But you're not going to settle for a life with just any man. You want your soul mate, your partner, and you can have him if you're loyal to these three beliefs:

- 🌸 I know what kind of man I want.
- 🌸 There's a life partner and a soul mate waiting for me.
- 🌸 I have the courage and the confidence to know I'll find him and we'll be married within a year.

Are You Playing Cinderella?

Our romance-focused culture makes us still believe in the knight in shining armor or in Cinderella and the Prince. We women always have difficulty saying, "I want to get married," because we believe in this Cinderella myth.

The more contemporary Cinderella story of the Prince and Princess of Wales shines greater light on our unreality. Princess

Diana was taken by surprise when the prince approached. He had his plan. He needed a wife and a mother for his children. He didn't need her to be his soul mate. He already had one. The princess was too young to have a plan. She was definitely not in control. She was taken by the temptation of being a real princess.

We've all succumbed to the Cinderella fantasy at some time. To overcome this fantasy, we must be in control of our lives. Often we're justifiably scared because we've had a bad first marriage or a painful relationship. In your heart you know a prince will not come and take you away to live happily ever after. Does this myth overpower you so that you feel you're a failure if you control your marital destiny? Do you believe you must be attractive enough, glamorous enough, and desirable enough to be pursued by this prince? Take control. Give up the myth.

Don't Sacrifice Your Essence

Soul mates don't sell their essence for lust or passion, or trade or compromise it for what appears to be a greater good. No greater good exists outside our essence. We are who we are and we want a partner who loves us for who we are. You can find him. You must trust in your essence and believe that he'll come to you when you're ready to send out your signals to him.

Your soul mate wants you as you are. Remember you are good and worthy of this love. He'll not want to change you.

Marriages that have two people who accept themselves as they are and love themselves have plenty of love. Each person feels secure enough in his or her own being to give love generously without hesitation or question. This inner sense of security makes for a strong foundation for their love to grow. This trust of oneself allows you to take risks, to challenge one another to greater growth. If we are mistrustful of ourselves, we tend to mistrust others. This mistrust can lead to pain and suffering and even greater insecurity about ourselves. Trust in who you are and you'll find trusting your partner is a wonderful gift that accompanies it. Love who you are and you'll find your partner will love you too.

From the beginning of a relationship believe in, trust in, and love yourself. If you sacrifice this self-love as the relationship gets under way, it will be very difficult to recapture it. Be true to who you are and what you want.

You Can Have What You Want

There's an old Irish saying: "Be careful of what you pray for because you'll get it." I'd like to reword that to say, "Be careful of what you desire because you can have it." If you want something then go after it. You'll get it. I've believed this for over twenty-five years and it has been successful for me.

Most of us have had a family, school, college, or work experience that challenged our healthy self-concept. You may have had a father or mother or ex-spouse or teacher who helped you to belittle yourself. You may need to work on erasing those belittling messages. You may still be reinforcing them. Do you trust yourself to love? Do you trust yourself to expect the best for yourself? Do you trust yourself to be happy? You deserve the best. Keep saying to yourself as you go through this goal-setting process, "I deserve and can have the best."

When I set my goal, my fears about dating were strong. I'd been dating only one person for three years. It was scary to get back out there and get in that game again. I soon began to think that I was getting too old. I didn't feel that way about myself but I was afraid that's how others would see me. I thought my chances of meeting someone who would want me were very slight, that "the good ones were all taken." I've learned that no matter what our circumstances, we all underestimate our self-worth. We must overcome our fears, our negative self-talk, if we want to meet our life mate.

Meeting as many people as I do through my public speeches, I've heard many destructive self-messages about the odds of getting married. "I'm too fat." "I'm not exciting enough." "I'm not interested in having someone else run my life." "I'm too selfish." "I'm too set in my ways." "I'm too tall." "I don't have enough money." "I'm not well educated." I'm sure you can add your own messages to this list. These are negative messages. They are excuses for not going after what we want. We need to challenge these messages and recognize where they come from. In most cases they spring from fear. If we overcome the fear of getting what we want, we can have it. If we want to get married, we can.

Set Your Goal

You too can get married according to *The Marriage Plan*. You can set a goal to get married. You can set a deadline to be married even without a potential mate in your life. Do you doubt me? Are you thinking you can't set a date without somebody in your life? That your family and friends will think you're desperate or crazy?

Most women don't have a plan to get married. They fall in love then decide on whether the fit is right. It's too late when they're emotionally hooked and can't make a reasonable judgment on whether that mate is good for them. If they're unsure it's because the inner soul is telling them the relationship isn't good for them but they're afraid to lose what they have.

Have you been involved in such a relationship? You got hooked emotionally, had sex, spent weeks, months, maybe even years together, and then fell apart. Was it you? Was it him? Did either or both of you find someone else to get hooked on temporarily?

Are you dating someone now? Are you crazy about him but aren't willing to say so because you don't know where his head is? You want to get married but you're afraid to take control, even mentally, of planning your life.

Are you single for a long period of time because you can't seem to find the "right" mate? Have you ever clearly defined what is right for you? Have you taken control of what will make you happy? Are you still playing Cinderella waiting for your prince who never comes? Are you too embarrassed to admit that you want to be happily married?

Are you single and looking but admitting this only to yourself? Why wouldn't you dare admit it to men friends or even to your best woman friend or to your family? Why are we embarrassed to admit that married life is for us? Why are we afraid of being in control of getting what we want? Why don't we take control of our future?

Karen, a young woman from Dallas in one of my goal-setting classes, had been living with her lover for two years. She always wanted to get married but had been playing the waiting game with him. The third day of the class she decided that that very night she'd tell him how she felt and either get a commitment out of him to get married or end the relationship. It was a risk she took but she decided that marriage was important to her. Her partner thought she was happy with their relationship as it was and was surprised to hear that she wanted to get married. Fortunately he was open to the idea of getting married. They talked it over and set a date. The following day she came to class and announced that she was to be married by the end of the month.

It's difficult to set personal goals for ourselves. If we set the goal and don't make it, we see ourselves as a failure. Sometimes we're even afraid of success. If we get what we want, we will have to change our lives.

Perhaps you've found success in your career but can't seem to find a happy relationship in your personal life. You've probably set lots of goals in your work life. Often those who have goal-setting experiences never connect that they can and should set goals for their personal lives. Setting goals for your personal life will keep you in control. It'll allow you to practice the discipline to know what you want out of life and to go after it. It'll make you responsible for your life and what happens to you. If you don't set goals, you may never have to worry about this responsibility. As the years slip by without personal fulfillment, you may blame others for your unhappy state. Is this the future you want?

Goals are meaningless without time deadlines. In business when we set a goal we always attach a date by which it will be accomplished. In the next chapter we will discuss the importance of setting a deadline for our marriage goal.

STEP TWO: SET A DEADLINE

Setting the Date Gives
You the Power

Be sure of the date and the mate. Accept nothing
less. Setting your goal and committing to your plan
will get you what you want. When you set your
date, things will fall into place. Your mate will get the
signals you send and events will happen so that you
and your mate can come together at the same time
and with the same intention, to be happily married.
Focus and desire cause things to happen because they
have great power to organize your life.

The couples in this book verify that knowing what they wanted helped them to recognize it when it came into their lives. Paul knew that he was on that path. All his actions were oriented to finding someone to marry and settle down.

I'd just ended my relationship with my fiancée, Shelley, when I began dating Jessie. I wanted to get married. Throughout my adult life I imagined myself as a husband and father and I worked at making it happen. I knew from the beginning that I wanted a partner, and Jessie and I are that.

I didn't write out the criteria for the person I wanted to marry but I did have them. What attracted me to Jessie was that I wanted someone with a similar education, and who was a business professional. I wanted somebody who had a high degree of independence, who could be a partner, who wouldn't dominate me or expect to be dominated or told what to do or how to do it.

Brenda actually got married according to goals she set before her second marriage. She had four criteria. "I wanted a man who accepted my children, was kind to me, had a good job and a secure future. I was clear that I didn't have to be in love with him. I was nuts about Ken and look what it got me." One criterion that she thought was not important to her was to be in love. She felt that when she was in love, love failed her. She was wrong. She met her deadline but because her goals were incomplete and not clearly thought out, her second marriage was a failure. Brenda believes that the failure of that marriage was actual proof that when *The Marriage Plan* is followed and well thought out, it works. People who set goals in other areas of their lives know that they get the results they set out to get simply because they desire and focus on them. They don't control all the circumstances that make the events happen but the results still come.

What is amazing about our nervous systems, our emotions, our brain is that we can "command" this organizing power through conscious goal setting. This goal is desire firmed up by belief it will happen. If our faith isn't strong enough, if we're selfish in our desires, if we don't trust in our influence on what happens in our world, and if we get attached to the details of our plan rather than to the outcome, our goal will get blocked.

Be Detached from the Details

Focus on the date but don't be attached to your plan exactly as you make it. It will not be fulfilled exactly as you lay it out. Be aware that you can be so attached to the details that you'll be blind to the events that will create your goal. You'll recall in my story how I set the rule of excluding divorced men from my pool of eligible mates. If I had become too attached to that rule, I'd have missed Robert.

I also was attached to my own plan of staying in Michigan when events were inviting me to Florida. The layoff from General Motors was an event I was fighting. Without my friend Helen to remind me that Divine Providence was working whether I understood it or not, I might have thrown away that opportunity. I needed to detach myself not from my goal but from how I figured my plan would work out. When we struggle against the happenings of the present because we're attached to a detail, we miss wonderful opportunities.

Jan, a woman acquaintance of mine, had heard of the success

of *The Plan*. She felt like she had set her goal to be married and also that she had picked the man to marry. Her plan was to strategize how to marry this man. This wouldn't have been a problem except she didn't know him. I listened carefully to her story. She had set her sights on a successful man whom she saw only once. She wanted to be happy but she attached her goal to this unknown man. She didn't free herself to allow happiness and love to come to her. Her determination blinded her to allow the universe, Divine Providence, to act through her. She may get the man but will she get her soul mate?

Phil, a man in one of my seminars, made arrangements to meet Deborah, with whom he had been "talking" online for months. He just knew she was his soul mate. When they met, things didn't go well. He continued to pursue it. He wanted it to work but she didn't. He became attached to one woman to fulfill his goal and he wasted time. When the flow isn't right, move on. Don't try to "fix it" to make it work.

When you set your date, you must believe that it'll happen. Take advantage of opportunities. Don't let doubts overcome you. Remain detached from *how* it's going to happen. And then, go with the flow and enjoy it.

Timing Is Everything

Finding one's soul mate is first a matter of timing. There are plenty of soul mates out there for you but the one that will be yours has to be in the same frame of mind as you, ready and able to get married within a year. The timing is key.

No doubt you've had at least one love affair that has gone awry. A potential soul mate may have already passed in and out of your life. You want the best odds for a happy marriage within your time frame. That's why you must set your criteria, you must be sure of what you want. If you're not sure of the kind of man you want, how will you know when you meet him?

Some of your love affairs went awry because the man at the time wasn't ready or able to make a commitment. You may have had an affair with a married man who was unable and unwilling to make a commitment to you. Or you may have had an affair with a man who was able but not willing. In most cases we women drag these affairs out too long. We're so in love with the adventure, the lust, or the passion, that we can't seem to call it quits until we get hurt. We're not in control of our emotions, our desires, and our love. Why didn't he want to marry you? Probably because the timing was off for both of you. He wasn't ready for commitment to marriage. He may have had things to do before he could commit. Some men just aren't ready when we are or we when they are. When this happens, accept it. It's impossible to make someone feel something they don't. Soul mates have to be at the same place at the same time. If not, you're not soul mates and you have to move on.

It's very helpful to write your date down; to see it on paper affirms it, makes it real. It's scary to write it down but you'll not be sure that you own this desire, this goal, until you do.

Set the Date

We *must* set deadlines or there's no goal to set. "How can I set a deadline when there isn't even anyone in my life?" you might ask. If you're in control, you set the time. Your mate will receive your signal when he's ready.

My daughter recently set a goal to get married. She decided that she wanted to be married by a certain date. She'd like to have a child and the time frame is critical for her. She's presently working at her goal. My stepdaughter also set a goal to get married. She gave herself two years. She also wanted to start a family. After she met the man of her dreams, she was firm on reaching her autumn marriage date, which she did. I believe she could have done it earlier but she wasn't confident enough in her own ability to meet someone and fall in love. Both of these women have successful careers and felt that they were missing the intimacy of marriage. They recognized that work isn't all there is to life. They wanted more.

How long do you think it should reasonably take you to meet a mate, fall in love, and marry? Most people can agree that a year seems reasonable. There may be rare exceptions but the goal should never be set longer than a year for anyone twenty-five and older. Longer than that, and we're playing games either with ourselves or with the man. If you set this date and the man you're seeing cannot agree to work within that time frame, then drop him. If you agree to a longer time frame, recognize that you risk losing control of your own destiny. To let someone else take control of this deadline is submission. Fears that you'll lose this person need to be overcome. If you submit to another in this step, you'll rarely be able to gain the equality necessary in a marriage.

This book includes stories of successful marriages that happened in as short a time as seven weeks. Granted, this is an unusually short time for a courtship but it can be done. Most of the couples fall somewhere between six and fifteen months. Not one couple, once they began *The Marriage Plan*, took longer than a year to set a wedding date. Cindy and Cliff were married in five months; Aimée and Don took less than a year. Paul and Jessie and

Laura and Stan each set their date for less than a year but volunteered to change it because of another family wedding.

It's now time for you to set your date. To begin you must articulate two things. You have completed the first, the goal statement: "I want to get married." The second is to set the date within a year. Do you have the courage to set this date? You bought this book because you thought you wanted to get married. If you still believe you want to get married and that you can find your soul mate, you've got some work to do.

Complete this statement: "I want to get married by _____."

Fill in this date. Don't be afraid. You can do it. Remember, carefully select this date and make it within the year. It'll happen by that date if you follow *The Plan*.

Now that you have committed to being married within the next year it is time to determine what kind of man you want to marry. We are all different in our desires and our dreams. What kind of man will make you happy? What values do you hold so dear that you will not compromise them? In the next chapter you'll design the profile of the man who is your soul's complement.

STEP THREE: DRAW A PROFILE

What Will He Be Like?

What will the man you want to marry be like? After you set the goal to be married and set the date, the third step in *The Marriage Plan* is to determine a clear profile of the kind of man you want to marry.

All of us have our own image of what kind of mate we desire. Some of us like our men blond and blue-eyed, others of us like them tall, dark, and handsome. Some of us will want someone older than we are, sometimes by only a few years and sometimes by as much as ten or twenty years. Others would like him somewhat younger. Some of us have strong feelings about his being of our own ethnic group or race. Others will like the differences. Because of our upbringing or the importance of our religious beliefs, some of us will choose not to marry outside our religion. If we've had a difficult time financially, we may be firm about looking for financial security in our partner. Before you answer this question of what kind of man you want to marry, let's visit with one of the women in our couples to see what she had in mind.

When Aimée set her goals, she had only been out with Don once and she hadn't looked at him as a possibility when she was setting her goal. Aimée had two long-term relationships in addition to her first marriage in which her children were born. She didn't want for dates. Men seemed to always be available to her.

I had breakfast with Aimée, a beautiful redhead, in New York City at a conference we both were attending. She and I had talked on the phone several times about her life. She was looking for a long-term relationship, she told me. I handed her a pad and pencil and said, "Write down 'I want to get married.' "

She handed it back to me saying, "Wait a minute. This isn't exactly what I had in mind. We didn't say anything about marriage. You told me that you would help me meet a wonderful man."

"If you don't have that goal in mind, then we don't have anything to talk about."

"Well, maybe I do want to get married. I don't want to go through the process every two or three years of meeting somebody, dating him, and getting to know him. It gets boring after a while." She wrote down the statement "I want to get married."

My next question, of course, was "When?"

"Three or four years from now."

I knew she felt she had to spend that long with someone before she knew him. Timing is very important in *The Marriage Plan*. If you put marriage off for three or four years, it isn't a priority.

"That's too long. It's got to be a short-term goal, not a long-term."

"I feel that I have to meet someone and get to know that person before I marry him. How long a goal can it be?"

"Not more than a year."

"I only have a year to get to know somebody? I don't have anybody in mind. I've been in one eight-year and one six-year relationship and I sure didn't know either of them in a year."

Aimée was beginning to show her irritation. I was expecting something from her, she thought, that she wasn't prepared to tackle.

"They weren't your soul mates either," I said.

Aimée said nothing for a while. Then she sat up straight, her eyes sparked, and she said:

"Give me the pen and paper. I'm going to do it by September 16 of next year, one year from this date. See this? This is a piece of paper from the Waldorf-Astoria. If this happens, I'm going to frame it. I'm just tired of dating. I lived with two different men and they both wanted to control me and it took me a while to get out of the relationships once I got into them. I certainly learned a lot about myself in those relationships. I need someone who will respect me for being me. I want someone who is financially stable, who will accept my children and make them feel comfortable when they come home to visit. My children didn't like the other men I was with."

She then set criteria for the man that she wanted to marry:

- He had to demonstrate to her that he had the capacity to love someone other than himself.
- He had to accept her adult children. They had to feel comfortable in the home Aimée and her future spouse would make.
- He had to accept Aimée as an independent person who would always have her own interests and career.
- She wanted them to be financially stable together.
- She wanted him to have his own interests.
- She wanted him to be affectionate and sexually compatible.
- She wanted him to not be controlling.

I then asked her about physical attraction. She had no criteria. "I'm sick of men who are narcissistic. I want a real man. I don't care what he looks like. I'm five nine; I'd like him to be that tall but, you know, it doesn't matter."

"What about age?"

"He has to be mature. I don't want a person who hasn't experienced life."

"What about religion, or race, or ethnic background?"

"I'm open. If I can find a man who fits all these criteria, I won't have to worry about any of those things."

"What about children? Can he have children?"

"Of course. I have children. I'd like him to understand what it means to have children."

"Aimée, you won't have trouble finding this man," I said. "You're beautiful both inside and out. You seem sure of yourself. You're open. You've put very few prescriptions on your ideal man. I know you'll be married by this time next year." At this point Aimée and I parted, promising to keep in touch by telephone so I could support her in working her plan.

Core Values

A core value is something so important to you that it defines who you are. It's part of your essence. If you're looking for a soul mate, then you must seek someone whose core values match yours. The most important core value, being in control of your own values, will lay the foundation for your marriage.

Don had learned much about himself in the years before his marriage to Aimée and was determined to find a woman with similar values.

I had so many disastrous relationships in my life that I decided I had to learn about the women before I actually dated them. So I decided to always take a potential woman partner to lunch to get to know her better.

I'd first talk about myself, my childhood and the effect it had on the women I was attracted to. I'd then ask her about her relationship with her mother and father. I had some criteria. I wanted a woman who was in touch with her feelings, who could love and express love, who was emotionally available instead of like those who hid their emotions. I found all of these when I found Aimée.

Neither Don nor Aimée focused on external characteristics. They focused on core values. It's all right to have criteria that are external but the most important ones deal with character.

Intimacy in courtship forms a bond between the man and woman. They share secrets. They don't judge each other. They develop respect for each other's essence and have neither the desire nor intention to change their mate. They communicate their past pain. They're open about what is important to them and what they'll not compromise. Later, we'll discuss the importance of intimacy in a relationship of soul mates. For now understand that intimacy is one of the core values that will bring you happiness and fulfillment.

For many people sharing a religion is a core value. The religion they practice is so important to them that they want someone who understands, respects, and even believes in the faith that they've undertaken. If they intend to have children, they want their children to be raised in this faith. If you feel this strongly about your religion, then you'll list this as a core value. It may have already occurred to you that these core values will give you some direction in which you might find your future partner. Johnny and Brenda have a strong religious belief. They share this in their daily lives and in assisting youth in their church. Although this wasn't essential for Brenda when she met Johnny, it was for Johnny and is for Brenda today.

Another core value is openness in communication. Most authors today describe open communication as an essential part of intimacy and happiness. Openness in communication is essential not only for a happy marriage but also for an effective courtship. It's one of the characteristics common among happy couples. This openness enables them to develop intimacy.

Does this mean you'll always have open communication? No, but it means that if you hold it as a joint value you'll work at it. Will you slip? Yes. Will you forgive and be forgiven? Yes. Forgiveness is possible when both share values based on respect, honesty, and love.

INTEGRITY

It's often difficult to distinguish between honesty and integrity. Both have in common a respect for truth. I know integrity as wholeness, keeping myself together, understanding and respecting who I am and the gifts I have. Sometimes it's difficult to know and understand my essence, but when I do, I don't want someone to steal it from me.

Often we'll say that someone doesn't "have it together." By that we mean that she or he isn't in control. They make poor judgments in relationships, in their careers, and with their friends and family. They say things they don't mean and do things they regret. Often they're filled with guilt and shame and aren't truthful with themselves. They have little or no integrity because they're not in touch with their essence. They want to be, but they simply don't know how to get in touch with their inner being.

All of us feel this way at times. In such situations either we manage to pull ourselves together or we get some help. It's important to be a "together" person when choosing to get married. Do you know your essence, what you want, and what kind of person you need to help you to grow in happiness? Do you know your very basic desires, your core beliefs and values about life? True, we all strive to mature and develop as each year passes, to get better at making judgments and choices, to know ourselves at a deeper level. But integrity is in the now, how we handle each day's basic, mundane tasks and crises.

I like all my choices to preserve my integrity. I like classical music but only when it speaks to my soul; it's rarely integral to my being. For my husband, Robert, all music speaks to his soul. He loves it in all forms and feels deprived if he cannot have it when he wants it. He loves films. They're a part of what turns on his energy and connects with his being. If he didn't have movies, he'd feel deprived.

If I were to ask him to give up his music or his films, I'd be asking him to give up part of who he is. Because they're less a part of me than they are of him, I might think he should compromise and not listen or watch these as much as he does. If I ask him to compromise something so important to him, then I'm asking him to sacrifice an important part of his integrity. He may have to give up some of this for other things that include me and he'd willingly do this. We need to be careful what we ask another to compromise if it's so much a part of who they are. We also need to be careful of compromising who we are for others.

Integrity is being in harmony with what we believe. If we believe women are full and equal partners in a marriage, then we'll make sure that our marriage reflects that belief. If we believe that our children are best raised by us rather than with a day care worker or a nanny, then we offer no apologies to anyone. If we believe that our life will be richer, our children happier, and our future more secure when we have a full-time career, then we do what we believe is right. We're true to what we believe.

Perhaps you're saying, "Fine and good, but we can't always do what we believe is right." Integrity is being true to our values, as honestly as we believe our lives will allow. If our finances as a single mother don't allow us to act out our beliefs to stay at home when we think we should, our integrity will help us choose how to make the best of the situation. We'll make great effort to assure that our child is cared for in the best way that we can provide.

Integrity is not only knowing ourselves and what we value; it's preserving those values at all times. We should not compromise who we are when we fall madly in love. We should not compromise our desire to get married or our values by accepting someone who doesn't meet our critical criteria. Being in love will not conquer all; in fact it could sometimes drain away our very essence. If we believe in who we are, then all our important choices and decisions will be measured against our true desires, beliefs, and goals. When we do this, we know we're preserving our essence, our wholeness, and our integrity. Only then will we be a truly together person.

Integrity, wholeness, is also important to recognize in your mate. Is he a person who believes in himself and in his values? Does he possess a character that shows you he can always count on being true to himself? Does he compromise himself when he is challenged by people who have control over him or whom he admires? Does he demonstrate respect for other people or does he denigrate them, disrespect their property, or act irresponsibly toward them? Most important, how does he relate to you in matters of integrity?

HONESTY

Honesty begins with recognizing who we are and then being truthful to ourselves. Self-honesty is based on integrity. It's admitting our strengths, our talents, our desires, and our feelings to ourselves. Being able to say "I'm a good accountant" is often easier than saying "I'm a good friend." These are both strengths. In our goal-setting workshops we have an exercise where we ask the participants to list twenty-five of their strengths. We give them ten minutes to think about it and then we give them five minutes to write down their twenty-five strengths. Some people never get to five. A few more get to ten or twelve. Less than 20 percent of the class ever reach twenty-five.

Most of us don't have the opportunity to admit our strengths and talents to ourselves. Do the exercise below to check out how honest you are with yourself. Give yourself five minutes to write as many strengths as you can. Your goal is to get to twenty-five. You can list anything from being a good skier to being a great lover. You can cite being responsible, trustworthy, caring, or assertive. This exercise will help you know and be honest with yourself, a crucial part of finding your true soul mate.

1.	14.
2.	15.
3.	16.
4.	17.
5.	18.
6.	19.
7.	20.
8.	21.
9.	22.
10.	23.
11.	24.
12.	25.
13.	

We try not to do an exercise on our weaknesses. Actually most of our weaknesses are the reverse of our strengths. If we're nurturing, caring, and sensitive to others, we're probably too sensitive to the comments of others. If we're an assertive, take charge, action-oriented person, we may step on the toes of others. By concentrating on our strengths, we learn to control our weaknesses. By concentrating on our weaknesses, we become them. Remember, we become what we focus on.

Being honest with others means being truthful, direct, open, and forthright with them. When I was quite young, I learned that there was a big difference between being public and being honest. Being honest is to admit the truth when called upon or when a situation demands it. Being public is telling all you know when people don't necessarily have any business knowing. Don't confuse the two.

In an intimate relationship, telling the truth is important to loving and understanding who the other is. Loving and accepting the deepest feelings and desires that the other shares builds trust. One partner's honesty demands that the other pass no judgment but simply accept what the person says as real. Can we accept the foibles, mistakes, values, and desires of the other? Perhaps in the sharing we'll find we cannot, that we're not soul mates. It's much better to find our incompatibility earlier rather than later.

When we play games, are untruthful or tell lies or cheat, we usually are doing it because we're not willing to face the reality of who we are, who the other is, and who we might become together. We fear the other knowing our reality. We believe if we pretend to be something we're not, he might love us.

What about honesty and integrity in your mate? You must encourage it by being loving and nonjudgmental. When he begins to share his real self, his hopes, dreams, and goals, when he tells you about his fears, his bad experiences, his friends, his family, and his spirit, you'll know he's being honest.

We must believe that we're lovable in ourselves, for ourselves. We must realize that our soul mate can find us only when we're true to ourselves. When we're true to our integrity, to our self-honesty, it will be so much easier for him to recognize us.

CAPACITY TO LOVE

What attracts one personality to another is a mystery. What turns you on may not necessarily turn me on. However, the one personality characteristic that turns all of us on is the capacity to love, a quality not always identifiable early in a relationship. The capacity to love like many talents comes in different volume amounts. Some have a pint, some a quart, and some have a gallon. If you have a gallon and your partner has a pint, then both of you'll be dissatisfied. You may smother him with all you have to give. You may feel deprived with the little he has to give. Brenda's story about her second husband is a good example of two strikingly different capacities to love. Alex couldn't give. He wasn't able to love her children. Brenda gives generously of herself. If someone can return that love, as Johnny has done, then she'll be fulfilled.

Signs of capacity to love are selflessness, generosity, affection, caring, thoughtfulness, willingness to accept love, to be open with you, and to talk about all subjects important to both of you. A person who withholds these important qualities may not be a match for you.

Not only is communication essential for a good marriage but it must be present in our premarital relationships also. If your potential mate plays his cards close to his chest, then the red flag should go up. Remember, the key for finding your mate is for you to not make excuses for behavior that's dangerous. We don't want you to confuse a quiet personality with taciturn behavior. Some people are naturally quiet. They need time to trust and to open up. Others, whom we should be aware of, may simply be antisocial. It's up to you to determine how much time that you'll give them. Remember, however, the courtship shouldn't be planned to go beyond a year.

Laura tells us that we cannot judge one's capacity to love by one's openness with other people.

> Stan's a lot more friendly and open than he used to be. It was hard for him to talk about personal things and I got him to talk about that. I don't tell everybody my business but I tell it like it is. And he's gotten to be that way as well.

Laura's ex-husband got seriously ill and was unable to care for himself. She felt obligated to care for him and did so for several months until he died. Stan felt that her willingness to care for her sick ex-husband, even though his alcoholism had caused Laura much pain during the years of their marriage, wasn't a threat to him but was a sign of her great capacity to forgive. Laura saw Stan's not being threatened as a sign of his great love. Caring for another brought them closer together. She also recognized Stan as a man capable of great love when she observed his care for his own family.

> Stan's got a great capacity to love. He's got four kids, six grandsons, and a brother. He's a very thoughtful person and has room for all of us. He's very affectionate. Without

this affection I don't think that you have a base. It nurtures the marriage. I value that very much.

Aimée and Don determined each other's capacity to love by watching the other's behavior outside of their relationship. Aimée's behavior with her children indicated how much she cared for them. One of her top criteria for a mate was that he accept and respect her children. Don observed Aimée's generosity with her friends. He noted that women seemed to like Aimée.

One of the ways that I knew the fullness of Aimée's capacity to love was watching her relate to other people. She'd always seem to be happy and smiling when she was around her friends or talking to them on the telephone. She had this habit of saving wrapping paper and ribbon. I don't save anything so I wondered if she were miserly. Actually I found she was very generous with her friends. She'd always give them gifts and the paper was saved so that she'd always be prepared to do so.

Aimée, in turn, was touched by Don's sensitivity.

One Saturday night he called to ask me out that evening. I had a date. I let him know if he wanted to continue to date me he'd have to give more notice. He'd have to plan better. So he asked me if I'd go to a movie the next night. This date was a turning point in our relationship.

I was subtly picking at him and criticizing him during the evening. After the movie he asked me to come back to his house. He went to his bedroom and was gone for some time. When he returned to the living room, he had a list with him. "I wrote down all the things you said to me tonight that hurt me."

I was totally embarrassed, apologized, and explained to him why I acted that way. From that night we were direct and honest with each other about our feelings. When we have something to say that might hurt the other person, we try to be sensitive and caring. I was so touched that, as hurt as he was, he didn't lash out at me. Even with the list he wasn't critical or judgmental. I began to fall in love.

In Johnny's caring and compassion for others in his life Brenda recognized a true capacity to love.

He'd stay with my mother when she was ill; go over to his mother's house and empty her trash; help my father and my kids when they needed help. I liked that he'd help his mother. I knew he'd understand how I felt about my mother.

Perhaps the most important sign of a mate's capacity to love is the ability and willingness to accept us as we are. We all have our idiosyncrasies and they are hard for others to accept. If someone is willing to put up with our quirks, then indeed he may have a great capacity to love. Paul recognized that Jessie accepted him for all of his.

Jessie has a great capacity to love. I believed it when I knew her patience should have been tried. I'd do foolish things from time to time and she was there just the same.

My husband, Robert, has this great capacity to love. Not only is he affectionate and loving (Italians love to hug) but he's a very giving person. I recognized this early in the way that he cared for his children and I've experienced it hundreds of times since. I'm a person who, although well educated, could be called flaky because I have a tendency to lose or misplace things. He's never failed to stop what he's doing to help me find something. I do get lectures now and then about being more careful but they are never in anger. It's this kind of love that tells me that he accepts me as I am.

If the man you're seriously considering marrying doesn't have the capacity to love that you need, then he isn't your soul mate.

ATTITUDES TOWARD EQUALITY IN MARRIAGE

The issue of equality in marriage is central to your expectations for a happy marriage. What is equality? Equality means that both husband and wife give each other the same portion of authority, responsibility, and accountability in the marriage and family. It means that each recognizes the talents of the other and respects the other's expertise in certain areas. It isn't based on prejudice of sex, power, physical prowess, or other stereotypes.

Everyone isn't equal in talents, abilities, intelligence, money-making power, or education. The clue to equality is respect and recognition of the talents you have and the expectations you have for your future spouse to respect these talents. What respect do you have for your partner's talents?

Each of the partners interviewed individually was asked two

questions about equality in their marriage. The first question: "Is yours a marriage of equals?" The second question: "Who has more control in your marriage?"

Cliff believes that he and Cindy have an equal partnership.

I think that we both have a lot of power in the marriage and neither of us feels powerless. It's whoever wants to allow the other one to dominate that particular day. Somebody has to make decisions to function. We do that on a basis that's comfortable for both.

Cindy evidently agrees with his interpretations since she believes that marriage has made her free.

Being married to Cliff has made me feel free to do anything I want to do. I'm surprised when women think otherwise. I think it sets you free. It's been freedom in terms of pursuing my career, freedom in terms of doing anything I want to at home, to get any kind of help I need.

Although Brenda and Johnny both believe that their partnership is equal, Brenda believes that Johnny has more control.

Johnny will do anything he wants. When it comes to his going to social events that I want to attend, I only press if it's a political or business command performance. A lot of people think that I'm in control. I don't have people over to the house as much as I would if he liked doing it more. I'd like to do more social things.

Johnny certainly doesn't agree that he has more control. He believes they have no control issues in their marriage.

We have an interdependent relationship. We're dependent on each other. My life would be a monstrous void without her. I not only love her but I like her a lot. She's a school board member and very active in the community so I find her very interesting.

Even though a couple loves each other and respects the other for his or her talents and personality, there can still be issues in the marriage that are not resolved. If they're not critical to you, then live with them. It's worth doing so to have a soul mate.

Many people don't consider issues of equality in the passion of courtship. In my planning process I considered equality more an issue of respect for who I am. I understood that I had a strong personality. I knew I'd always have a career and recognized that my future spouse would have to respect that. This was a top priority for me. On the other hand, there weren't very many other issues I felt that strongly about. I was willing to move for his career as long as I could have mine.

Is having a career or a profession important to you? Jessie was involved in a previous marriage where her husband had expectations of her staying at home and raising a family rather than developing her career. Although she had never said or done anything to give him that expectation, he still had it. Although marriages break up for many reasons, that difference in expectation was the focal point for the breakup of their marriage.

Do you believe that your feelings about having or not having a career could be a problem for a potential mate? Does it take so much of your time that it would deprive you of the time a relationship might need? What is it you'll not give up? Would you move if your spouse's career demanded it? Is geography, where you make your home, important to you? Answer these questions forthrightly and as clearly as you can. When you meet your mate, it's important to discuss both your career values as well as career goals.

Another aspect of equality and independence in marriage is how you spend your leisure time. Do you have friends of the opposite sex that you expect your mate to understand will continue to be your friends? We're not talking about ex-lovers, necessarily, but simply men with whom you've developed a deep friendship. If this is the case, then you need to be prepared to test the feelings of your future mate about your friends of the opposite sex. Paul feels very strongly that people who have at one time been best friends should be able to continue to have a friendly relationship. He still speaks to his old girlfriends and remembers their birthdays. All of them have met his wife and children. Would you be comfortable if your spouse had these relationships?

I haven't raised all of the issues that could be critical to your concept for equality in marriage. That's something you must do for yourself. A word of caution: If you feel strongly about being in control in a marriage, then consider whether you can function in a marriage of equality. You may need to look for a partner who is willing to allow you to be the boss and that means you'll be looking for a man with that rare combination of passivity and a healthy self-concept. Recognize that many people who are outwardly passive are manipulative. If he doesn't get what he wants, you may get punished, sooner or later, in one way or another. Can you live with those consequences? Your answer will help you to decide on what is of value to you.

When you enter a relationship with self-respect and respect for your partner, you can expect to achieve equality in your marriage.

CHILDREN

Whether or not to have children is a major value that must be shared by both mates. Not only for the obvious reasons of cooperating in the conception but also in cooperating in the responsibility for raising the children. If both mates do not have the same desire to have children and to raise them, if both mates do not have the same values about how children should be raised, it's a catastrophe for the mates and the children that may be born within this dissonance. It is important for you to understand what you want and when.

How do you feel about having children? If you want children, you'll want to envision your soul mate as the father of your children. Are you clear about how long after marriage you want to start your family? When to have children is often a point of disagreement. Do you have time to decide or is your body clock already ticking? Are you willing to delay having children if he wishes? Are you willing to have them sooner if he wishes?

What expectations do you have for raising the children? Will you raise them full-time? Will you continue your career and use day care or a nanny? How much and in what way will you expect your husband to participate in the raising of the children?

How do you expect to be an equal partner if you care for the children full-time? What expectations do you have to assure your financial well-being? Two salaries are a substantial help in raising and educating children. What will each of you have to give up if only one salary is being earned?

Because the wife and mother has the primary responsibility to care for the children in the majority of households, are you willing and able to carry the burden as well as the joys?

Jessie and Paul faced difficulties with a two-career family. They struggled with each other as children broke into their circle of life. Jessie describes what it was like for her to keep a career and raise children:

I realized that by the time Maureen was five that I always had this picture of one, maybe two kids. I realized that as Paul kept asking for the second child that I wanted only one, especially after I found out how hard it was. I wouldn't consent until he agreed that he was going to spend more time helping me with them.

Once you have kids, it means a lot of responsibility, and it's been a struggle sometimes for me to let Paul play by himself. It's not at all unusual for him on the weekend to play trombone or in the summer to go sailing without me, which means I have the kids. When we didn't have kids, I couldn't care less. He helps a lot more with the kids than he used to but we still struggle with it.

There's only one time ever that I thought Paul would walk out. Maureen was about a year and half and I was unwilling to let up on things like bedtime at the same time and naps in the afternoon. It's a strain trying to take care of a little toddler when you're both pretty independent people with full careers. I said to Paul, "I can't do this by myself," and he responded, "If it means I have to do it the way you're doing it, I can't do it."

I stopped expecting him to help and raised Maureen my way. When we had Beth, he knew what he was getting into and he liked helping to care for her. Today it's a pretty good partnership.

Paul's account of these circumstances is slightly different.

I had to adjust to parenthood a lot more than Jessie did. I always saw myself as a father but I didn't realize what was involved. I tried to keep up my earlier lifestyle and it was impossible. I wanted to have the second child because I wanted Maureen to have a sibling. My mother was an only child and she told me how difficult it was being raised without a brother or sister. Jessie recognized how hard it would be for us to go through toddlerhood and babyhood all over again. Now we've gotten through that.

Paul learned how to become a contributing parent and a more understanding husband. Their children are young and their struggle isn't over.

Paul and Jessie's views are typical of the day-to-day struggles parents go through in raising children and complicated by both having high-powered careers. Even if the mother chooses to stay home, the father's participation is often an issue in a family. Mothers report that often their mates don't respect the fact that the mother has had the children all day and often all week, and that she needs help in the evening and on weekends.

You want to examine these issues and questions before you choose your mate because how you feel about children is an emotion that touches the soul and affects every desire and dream you've ever had. When completing the exercise at the end of this chapter, refer to these questions to be sure you've thought this through completely. Let your answers help you to direct these same questions to your potential mate early in the relationship.

STEPCHILDREN

How do you feel about marrying a man with children? If you have some strong negative opinions on this issue, stepchildren can be a major barrier to finding a mate. Often people don't understand that marriage is a commitment not just to one person but to a whole family. Would you be willing to take on the huge responsibility of getting to know children of any age and work at developing a relationship with them?

Susan tells us that she had some real difficulties in marrying someone with young children:

> They were so unstructured and so undisciplined that I found it very difficult to be around them. I remember we were in a store and the kids were all over the place. Sure enough one of them got lost and was crying. I just thought anything could have happened. Debbie, their mother, and Mark were both at times very blasé about things that I thought were very important.
>
> They just had a very different approach to raising them. It always felt like an invasion every time they would show up for the weekend. Mark wasn't good at managing their diet and their bedtime.
>
> They're turning out fabulous. I love them to pieces. They still make me crazy but if they were mine there would still be times in which they would make me crazy. Mark hated interacting with their mother. There was still a lot of scar tissue. Debbie was still very forceful with him and he never fought her on anything. His concern was al-

ways that she'd deny him access to the children. She didn't like being told no and he understood that.

Could you love a man so much that you could share in the raising of his family, even on a part-time basis? Children have the varieties of personalities, the same love and hate, anger and sweetness that characterize us adults. There is, however, one difference. We can walk away from adults we don't like. When we marry a family, walking away isn't an option unless we want to leave our mate.

I had some pretty strong feelings about marrying a divorced man with children. I believed that it would bring all kinds of challenges and problems that I didn't want. Of course my feelings about divorced men and other women's children were all based on fears of the worst that could happen. I was looking at the half-empty cup rather than the half-full one. Generally I was an optimistic person but somehow the fear of living with children overcame my rationality.

Then I met Robert. All the fears of living with and helping him raise his children were erased. Robert was very clear about how important his children were to him. He was also very clear with them on where he stood with me. He told them that as husband and wife we both came first with each other. "That doesn't mean," he said, "that I love you any less. I've lots of love to go around. It does mean, however, that I know you'll be testing whether I still love you and you'll be trying to make me choose you over Aggie. I won't do that."

We all agreed that it would be up to the girls and me to develop our own relationship. Robert wouldn't be my intermediary or theirs. With that ground rule, all of us started working to get along with each other. It worked so well for us that for Mary's twenty-fifth birthday, Robert and I adopted her legally, the best gift we could have given each other.

I thought I felt strongly about not being willing to raise someone else's children but I learned that sharing the raising of children was something I could accept. Equality in our marriage meant applying the same standards and conditions to raising the children. We agreed to respect each other's authority, not to contradict the other's rules or regulations with the children, and to discuss in private our disagreements that affected them.

Many divorced parents are not willing to share their children as Robert was. They're jealously possessive of their love. Often this possessiveness gets in the way of the marriage and the happiness of the children. On the other hand, many children will not accept the stepparent because they see it as disloyalty to their other parent. To eliminate these kinds of negative upbringing, everyone must be open to discussing their roles, their situations, and their respect for the absent parent. This is especially true of the adults in the situation. The parents must be the role models.

Stepchildren are involved in all but one of the marriages described in this book. All of the biological parents tell how important the acceptance of their children was to them. Stan, with four grown children, understood that introducing Laura, an only child with no children of her own, into a family this large could be traumatizing.

Laura had some apprehension about whether the kids would accept her but she didn't have any problem. She got closest to Rebecca, the youngest. Laura brought maturity to a relationship that Rebecca never had with her mother. She's picked up some habits of Laura's. Good ones.

Laura was very open to accepting Stan's family.

His daughter, Rebecca, asked me when we were first married how I felt about her mother. My answer was, "She's your mother and she'll always be your mother. She didn't want to be with your father any more and I'm glad to have him." Rebecca came over to Europe and spent time with me in the summers when I was there. We have developed a good relationship. She was daddy's little girl and I was the one who would have to say if she was out of line on some issue: "Just what do you think you're doing?" The boys, more reserved but never antagonistic, have come around over time.

Cindy and Cliff made an agreement to have one united front when it came to their relationship with their nine children, a number that would challenge the relationship of any couple. Cliff tells us:

I think we had problems with our children on both sides. Her oldest son, Daron, had been the man of the house for years. He had a tough time dealing with my taking over his place and still likes her full attention without any interference. He wants her to cook things for him, and do other things that assure him that his mother's still his mother. I know exactly when it's going to happen and I just get out of the way. Because of that he and I've become very close. It took a lot to get to that point.

With the girls, it's a whole different story. I came on the scene when Marsha was going through those rebellious puberty years. Now we're as close as father and daughter can be. I probably talk to her almost more than her mother does. She appreciates that and it helps her a lot. Ellen was nearly eight when we married and I'm the only father that she remembers and loves.

Some of my kids like Cindy more than others do because she's spent a lot of time with some of them. Right now they all understand our relationship. We always spoke with one voice. That's how we've survived the attacks. If we had anything we disagreed on, we discussed it until we came to a mutual decision before we talked with the children.

Don feels Aimée brought him closer to his children.

I have two grown daughters. They like Aimée and, actually, my time with them has gotten better since Aimée has been with them. She relates very well to women. I like her son and daughters and have developed a good relationship with them.

At our marriage we had a special part of the ceremony for our children to come forward. The minister asked them if they would support us in our marriage and not do anything to harm our relationship. We were all very happy about this inclusion.

I've met so many men and women who share the fear of becoming involved with a man or woman with children. It can be a special gift that your potential spouse will be giving you. Don't shy away until you've met all the parties and know whether it's something you not only can live with but also might indeed truly consider a gift. Don't deprive yourself of an opportunity out of fear.

Raising stepchildren isn't always easy, but neither is raising your own biological children. Parents make mistakes, stepparents also make mistakes, and, yes, children make mistakes. All need to be willing to forgive and to show mercy. For without mercy and forgiveness, there's no love.

MOTHERS OF STEPCHILDREN

For many second wives, dealing with the mothers of stepchildren is often a difficult encounter. Old feelings run deep. Even if the ex-wife wanted the divorce, she may still have mixed emotions about her former husband remarrying and "another woman" moving into her family. She may see you as the enemy and treat you as such. If your husband has any guilt about the divorce, he too may have mixed emotions about your participation with his children. If both of these conditions exist, you'll be taking on a very complex problem.

Let's deal first with the ex-wife. The real question is, Can you communicate with her? If so, then it would be helpful to come to an agreement between the two of you for the sake of the children. That should include the following points:

- Neither of you will speak poorly of the other in the presence of the children.
- You will always be civilized with each other.
- She will not speak poorly of your husband in your presence.
- Both of you will have rules for the children in your respective homes and you both will support the other's discipline.

This agreement, of course, assumes that you can talk to each other like civilized human beings. It should take place before you marry but after the commitment between you and your soul mate. Suppose the conversation doesn't go well and no agreement can be reached. It's then up to you to let her know that the children's well-being will always be a priority with you and you'll still try to keep your side of the agreement.

At the end of this chapter you'll answer several questions regarding the issue of children in a relationship. Be sure to consider this issue and all the core values very carefully. Understanding your feelings, making sure that your soul mate shares his with you, and each of you considering the other's is imperative. For now let's turn our attention to some external characteristics in your potential mate.

External Characteristics

PHYSICAL ATTRACTION

We twentieth-century Westerners put high value on marrying for love. We believe that physical chemistry makes a happy marriage. For thousands of years, however, our ancestors put less value on physical attraction and falling in love than we do. Marriage was an economic matter. People married to increase their social and financial worth. Even the poor arranged marriages for the survival of families. All of the couples in this book followed our current value system; they set out to marry for love.

Physical attraction, or chemistry, is important. But many readers, young and old, have made, or will make, the mistake of believing that physical good looks are of prime importance when searching for a mate. Good looks help in physical attraction, certainly. Nevertheless, oftentimes the tall, dark, and handsome or even the blond and just average handsome man has little capacity for love. The same is true for buxom blondes or petite, cute redheads. Be open to all physical attraction, not just conventional good looks. Beauty does come from the soul, and the personality is its mirror. These aspects of one's character will last a lifetime.

Physical attraction can be short-lived but there's an element of physical attractiveness that doesn't fade with the years, namely respect for one's body, for how it looks and the care it gets. Good physical health and a good mental attitude contribute more to physical attractiveness than beauty.

Only two people from our couples, one man and one woman, mentioned the physical beauty of their mates. To me Robert was very handsome and I was immediately physically attracted to him. Cliff thought Cindy was "gorgeous" and was immediately turned on by her looks. Generally the couples in our stories valued physical beauty less than their partner's inner qualities.

Attraction is important but it is not the total person. Physical attraction prepares to be attracted to the soul. Remember not to overestimate physical attraction when you are writing your criteria.

FINANCIAL SECURITY

Does he have to have money? This question focuses on the number one problem in marriages: finances. The saying "We don't live on love alone" is true. Many couples, however, consider themselves to be poor financially but are truly happy. There are many couples who live unhappy lives yet have all the riches one could desire. The question we want to focus on here is, How do we get happiness and live a successful life?

You must determine the standard that's important to you. When I was making my plan, my age and my own ambitions for a career dictated my answers. It wasn't important that he be rich, but he did have to have a job. This was true for the women we interviewed. They wanted independent, self-reliant mates who had good jobs. For me, he had to be ambitious in his chosen field. He didn't have to want to go to the top but he'd have to want to improve his position. I didn't want to be the sole breadwinner.

All of the couples in this book sought and attained financial stability through hard work. You'll have to consider your age, your financial well-being, assets and liabilities, your family situation, and any other serious financial obligations when you determine your financial values. We're not advocating that you be a gold digger, but neither do you want one for a partner. Nor do we support a life of poverty. Set some goals for what basic financial situation would make you happy.

Before Cindy and Cliff got married, they didn't discuss finances. Like so many people, financial security was left to the post-wedding discussions. Cindy knew that Cliff had a successful business as a mason contractor and Cliff knew that Cindy was a successful businesswoman. This knowledge, however, didn't solve their financial issues.

We didn't discuss finances before we were married. He takes care of the basic things like the mortgage payments, and I take care of everything else. He's very free with money and is extremely generous. If I asked him for five thousand dollars, he'd give it to me as soon as he could. But if I say, "Let's take five thousand dollars and invest it," he wouldn't. I have no idea how many hundred-dollar bills he carries. It's a security blanket for him and perhaps for many men it is. I wish I had figured out earlier about his not trusting his money to investments; I'd have taken control of our investments a lot sooner.

The first time we went to the financial planner Cliff sat there with his arms folded; he just wouldn't talk about investing money. I plan for our financial future. He's very well protected if something happens to me and I'm financially secure if something happens to him. Does he have a need for control of money? Yes, but only with cash. He doesn't care about any other kinds of control.

For some people, financial security is a core value. They want their mate to have sufficient money or a secure job so that finances will not be a problem between them. They believe that they too should have their own independent source of money. For many women this means that they intend to work and control their own money. This is often not as important an issue with men since they generally assume that they'll be the provider of the family. Aimée discusses this aspect of their marriage:

We had a difficult time over money. In the beginning Don wanted to be in control of our finances. He had everything on the computer, running a cash flow analysis twice a day. I was used to handling all my own finances in business as well as in my personal relationships. I think money can give someone more power over another. I think that it's important that power play isn't available in the relationship. If you're going to share your life together, it's important to share everything.

We decided it would be our money, not his or mine. He'd put our finances on the computer.

The first year was tough financially because the business market changed for both of us. A lot of our relationship was about finances because neither of us was making the kind of money we were used to. Don isn't a selfish person. If he had an unlimited supply of money, he'd give it to me. We've been making compromises about our situation and have come out of it with a deeper relationship. It was a matter of building trust with each other.

Money is often a source of power and control for many people. They don't want someone else to have so much power over them that they become defenseless and helpless in the marriage. Aimée tells us of this fear:

It was very important to me not to be with a controlling mate. I had been with very controlling men in my past, especially when it came to money. I lost my power in those relationships. That has not been the case with Don. I'm my own person. In a relationship where you can discuss finances, you can arrive at compromises. Sometimes fear of losing our own control makes us want to control others' lives.

Because it's a source of so many problems in a marriage, be very clear on how you feel about money and financial security. What do you expect from your mate? Do you expect all your money to be put in the same pot and both of you have equal control? Do you expect to have an equal say in how all your money is spent as a family? Brenda describes the different values that she and Johnny have about money:

> The first time I ever went shopping with Johnny I paid eight dollars for a glass. He said, "Why would you pay eight dollars for a glass which is going to break?" I said, "Then we'll buy a new one."
>
> Our values about money are totally opposite. When we went to a therapist together we had to describe what money meant to us. To me money is like pebbles on a road. You pick them up and put them in your pocket and when you run out, you pick up some more. Money to him was the Rock of Gibraltar.

Johnny says that he's a poor manager of money but so is Brenda. They have joint accounts and both write checks out of them. Neither is very good at keeping track of what they spend. They disagree on the value of money and on how they look at it. They're lucky that money isn't tight in their budgets. If it were, what kind of disagreements might ensue?

Finally, Jessie tells us about the financial issues in their marriage:

> This is the one place that we've never had big problems. It's always been what's mine is yours, what's yours is mine. We've maintained separate checking accounts. He pays one of the mortgages, which is taken automatically out of the account every month, and the school taxes, which come only twice a year. I pay all others.

He never asks me and I never ask him what he does with his money. We consult each other on the big items.

He's very conservative, the opposite of my father who had difficulty making the checkbook balance every month. Paul takes a lot of time before he spends any money and labors over getting the best deal. I'm not like that although I don't necessarily spend a lot of money. Both of us have the same values of not having credit cards maxed out or being way overextended.

One of today's most common marital issues has to deal with what happens to a woman's independence if she chooses to stay home and take care of the children. It's also an issue for males who stay home and take care of the children. Whose money is it? Is it both of yours? Does the money earner believe that whoever makes it controls it? If so, what does such an attitude say to the prime caregiver at home? It's easy for the woman who remains at home to become valueless in her own eyes, to feel like a child being taken care of by a parent. Today, when so many women are choosing to stay at home with their children, couples often will agree on a joint account. She'll have as much authority over the use of money as he. Other couples have agreed that she'll be paid a salary for her work, usually 50 percent of the husband's income. If you agree that one of you will remain at home to care for the children, how will this be financially valued in your marriage?

Money is an important issue for most couples. It affects independence, autonomy, control, personal worth, and power. Whether you have quite a bit or very little will have a major impact on your relationship. Think about what money means to you as you select your criteria for your mate.

Will you respect your mate's feelings about controlling finances? Do you want to control them? Or, at the least, do you want to control your own? Money can definitely be a touchy subject in any relationship. Talking about it before the marriage can identify some of the issues. If the differences cannot be resolved, it may be a sign that this isn't your soul mate.

RACE AND ETHNICITY

What are your criteria for marrying within your own race or ethnicity? The answer to this question depends on many factors. You may live in a geographical region or a large urban area where interracial or interethnic marriages are quite acceptable, even the norm. Or you may have grown up in a family that would make it very difficult for you to continue your relationship with someone if you married outside your own culture.

Is your core value on race and ethnicity something you believe in or is it something that has been handed down in your family? Do you believe that you wouldn't be happy, or that it would be very difficult for you to be happy, if you married outside your race or ethnic group? There are many happy marriages of interracial or interethnic origins. Many generations ago people didn't marry outside their own religious orientation or even their own town. Many of those taboos have weakened in America in the last twenty years. In some families and cultures they've been eliminated.

Cliff tells us that he was brought up with such a taboo. "I never thought about race because I only saw myself with a black woman. It was established early in my life that a relationship outside of my race was a no-no. I don't know whether that's good or bad but that's just the way it was."

Jessie, who is white, was brought up with similar taboos. She said, "I just never thought about it. I never had the opportunity to date someone other than a white man so it never was an issue for me." Yet Cindy and Brenda, both of whom are African American, were open to dating anyone who met their criteria, no matter what their race. "We talked many times about being open to race. As black women we decided we should not be limited."

Your feelings on this issue are very critical for a happy relationship. If your feelings are exclusive then you must send out a clear message. You also will eliminate a large portion of the eligible population. This, however, isn't a barrier. If you have a desire and you're very clear, there will be a receptor no matter how small the potential population is.

Today Jews marry Christians. Muslims marry Hindus and Catholics marry Baptists. Many Asians marry Caucasians or other Asians of a different culture. There are happy marriages of African and European Americans or Hispanics and American Indians. The decision of limitation is up to you. Make it with a great deal of thought.

DIVORCE

In all of the couples' stories, one or both of the partners had been divorced. What are your feelings about marriage to a person who has been divorced? If you have some strong religious beliefs, this may eliminate many potential candidates. Do you have some unexamined prejudices about people who have been divorced? How do you weigh someone who has been divorced more than once? Do you accept one divorce but not two? Are you open to giving anyone who has been divorced a chance? Do you feel that someone who has been divorced more than once is a high risk for a successful marriage? How will you test these theories you may have?

Getting to know your potential mate will help you decide whether his divorce has affected him negatively. For some people a failed marriage can be a learning experience. If their self-concept has not been damaged, and they come out relatively strong, a good second partner in marriage may be all they need to be happy and to share happiness. For many others, a failed marriage destroys their self-concept and they need counseling help before they can be happy. Two of the women and one man in our couples found happiness after two divorces. Their previous marriages taught them what kind of person they wanted and needed. Although they approached the courtship with trepidation, they took a risk and the third time was a charm.

Whether you allow yourself to marry a divorced person should be based on knowledge of the person rather than the stereotype that I created for my profile. Unless you have a strong religious reason preventing you from marrying a divorced man, open your mind to the realities of divorce discussed above, and expand your opportunities for finding you soul mate.

EDUCATION

How educated do you want your spouse to be? May he be more educated than you are? If you have a high school diploma or none at all, will you feel intimidated by his or her Ph.D. or master's degree? Both equal and unequal educational backgrounds in marriages can be very competitive.

For Cliff education is very important.

What I've done is limited so I want people around me who are educated. I had to educate myself. To make money I had to compete with educated people. That's what I still do today. I had to take something I was good at and make a business out of it. But it's very important to me that people be educated.

I didn't necessarily have to have a woman who was educated but I had to have someone who was intelligent. My mother, although an alcoholic, was a strong woman who encouraged and inspired me to continue on under some very bad circumstances. That's the kind of woman I wanted.

Cindy put high value on education for herself. She got her college degree after she had her three children. She earned a master's degree after she married Cliff. Yet in Cliff she recognized a different kind of intelligence.

Our difference in formal education has never been a problem. Cliff is very bright. He can look at a blueprint of a building and know immediately how to build that building. He's logical and creative and trusts his intuitiveness better than any man I know.

I had no one criterion for education for my potential spouse. He did need to be fairly intelligent, and I wanted to be able to carry on an intelligent conversation with him. He needed to have his own interests, his own competencies, and his own job, career, or profession. It didn't matter what it was. He could be a laborer; my father was a carpenter. He could be a doctor or a lawyer. It wasn't important to me. What was important is that he not be intimidated by my education or career and that he respected and was good at what he did.

I realize that many people put a high priority on education. We have some friends who wouldn't think of dating someone who didn't have a level of education equal to theirs. We also have some happily married friends who have vastly different levels of education. She's a skilled orthopedic surgeon and he's a mechanic. Both are highly intelligent, love each other, have two small children, hearts of gold, and many interests.

Your personal experience will be your guide to the level of importance education has in picking a partner.

What Will You Not Compromise?

In his *Report on Male Intimacy*, Michael McGill writes that many men in his study have friendships outside of marriage. Many of them have longtime associations with women who are their friends. They're able to confide in these women. Some men have close male friends who are their confidants. Would you tolerate these associations if your future spouse valued these friendships or would they threaten you?

Do you have a hobby or a skill that's so important to you that you don't want to give it up? Some people find that their inner self is expressed in a hobby such as basketball, bowling, dancing, films, hiking, painting, music, or a myriad of different interests. Would you be threatened and ask your spouse to give up such hobbies if you can't or don't want to share in them? Paul says that his strong love of sailing became a problem for his wife after they had children because of the amount of time he gave to it. He also took out-of-town gigs with his band. It was difficult for Jessie to take all the burdens of the children when Paul went on these trips. They came to a compromise. Paul limited his trips with the band and took more responsibility for the children on the weekends. It could have been a crisis in their marriage but through persistent communication they were able to work it out.

Are you close to members of your family? What role do you expect your mate to play in interacting with them? Are you willing to distance yourself from or give up your family relationships if he doesn't like them? How much time will your family expect from you and your spouse? Can you control these relationships if you want to or if your spouse would ask you? Some of Cliff and Cindy's kids, both as young people and as grown adults, made many demands on their father and mother. Sometimes the burdens were psychological and sometimes they were financial but at all times Cliff and Cindy carried these burdens together. Johnny took care of his mother and Brenda's parents. What would have been your reaction if those demands were made on you?

All relationships demand both tolerance and compromise. If you couldn't be tolerant of, or compromise on, some issues, it's best to express them now. For example, if you can't tolerate smokers, then eliminate smokers from your potential mates.

Write down the things that you won't tolerate or compromise on. The list will be your guideline for eliminating prospective candidates.

1.

2.

3.

4.

5.

Now that we've discussed some important criteria for choosing a soul mate, it's time to do some hard work for your own plan. The exercises below will help you to isolate those expectations that are important to you in a mate. The last exercise is to draw a profile of your soul mate. It is this profile that will help you to meet your soul mate in a year. In the following chapter you will begin to practice the hardest of the steps, trusting that he is looking for you and that he will come into your life.

Exercise One: Core Values

Begin to write down your core values. Use the information in this chapter to guide you. Besides integrity, honesty, capacity to love, equality and children, what other core values do you have? Try not to exceed listing five beyond these general ones and be honest. Your future happiness depends on it.

Write out specific elements of each of these values that you want in your future spouse (e.g., Honesty: *I don't want him to lie to me*). What will he say or do to let you know that he has each of the values below? (For example, *He'll tell me the truth even under embarrassing circumstances.*)

Honesty: _____

Integrity: _____

Intelligence: _____

Trust: _____

Ability to Be Intimate: _____

Ability to Communicate: _____

Capacity to Love: _____

Flexibility: _____

Other Values: _____

Exercise Two: Equality and Control in Marriage

Answer the questions below. After you've finished, review each of your answers. Set priorities on what is critical to you. On which issues will you not compromise?

1. In which areas of your life together do you want equal control?

2. Identify the one element that you believe to be most important for your self-respect, the one issue that you wouldn't compromise.

3. State your opinion about two-career families.

4. Is your career as important, less important, or more important than your future mate's? Why?

5. How would you feel about giving up your career for the benefit of your spouse's success?

6. Would you move anywhere for your own or your spouse's career?

7. What do you believe is necessary for equality in a marriage?

8. Are there any other issues about which you would find it necessary to give equal weight in the marriage?

Now review all your answers. Are you willing to compromise on any of these issues? Which ones and in what ways will you compromise?

Exercise Three: Children and Stepchildren

Write a paragraph that describes your feelings about having your own children. Have you decided if you want children? How many? How will you raise them?

Write a paragraph about how you feel about marrying someone with children. Include how you feel you want to be treated by the stepchildren, how you would like to treat them, and how you would like your husband, your soul mate, to behave in the relationship that includes you, the children, and the children's mother (his ex-wife).

Exercise Four: External Characteristics

Answer these questions before you draw up your list of external characteristics that follows.

What age range? _____

What ethnic background? _____

What is my minimum criterion for financial security? _____
_____
_____

What physical characteristics are important to me? _____
_____
_____

Will I accept a divorced or widowed partner? _____
_____

Will I accept a partner with children? _____
_____

What religious or spiritual orientation must my partner have?
_____
_____

What level of education must my partner have? _____
_____

What line of work would I like my partner to be in? _____

_____

Make two lists, the first, your own external characteristics, the second, the external characteristics you want in your mate. Include physical attraction, financial security, religion, race or ethnicity, previous marriages, and education.

Mine: His:

Exercise Five:

List the Critical Characteristics

That You Cannot Tolerate in a Person

·

Review all five previous exercises and look at the profile you've drawn up. Are there any contradictions? How will you resolve them?

It is time to do the actual selection. Write a summarizing paragraph for Profile of My Mate below. Include issues that are important to you, equality, core values, external characteristics, and children.

Profile of My Mate

STEP FOUR: TRUST THAT HE'LL COME INTO YOUR LIFE

You've decided that you want to get married. You've decided a date by which you'll be married and you've selected a profile of the mate that you're going to marry. Now, how do you meet this man? Well, relax. The next step is easy.

Pick a quiet spot. With your goal statement and the date you set and your profile on your lap, envision sending these desires out to your future mate. Calm down. Don't fret about it. It will happen if you don't mistrust yourself. You must express your desire very clearly. State that you want to get married. Determine what you want in a marriage partner. Know and expect that you'll find it. Those desires go out beyond you. They reach out to your prospective mate and he picks up the signal. Be very clear about what signals you want to send.

Visioning Your Mate

Your future mate will be ready to receive the signals when you're ready to send them. You may not know your potential mate now. It doesn't matter; he'll pick up the signal. You need only to be clear about the message. Send it out and then trust and be alert to what happens.

"Are you saying that all I have to do is set my goal and send out my message mentally and it will happen?" you're probably asking. Yes, that's what I'm saying. Hold on. Don't close the book. Give me a chance and read on.

To remind you how powerful thoughts are I'm going to take you through an exercise. Think about a situation that makes you angry, or perhaps a person you dislike, are jealous of, or who totally irritates you. When you think about that situation or that person, what happens to your body? Your body responds emotionally. Are your hands clammy, or is your heart starting to beat rapidly? Is your stomach rolling or crunching?

Negative thoughts are *very* powerful. They're depressing and dysfunctional. They produce stress, anger, headaches, and erratic breathing. We're told negative thoughts can even produce heart attacks if you have enough of them over a very stressful period.

What about positive thoughts? Let's check out their power over us. Relax. Close your eyes and think about a vacation in the Caribbean. If you've never been there, imagine what it would be like. Are you ready? Are your eyes closed?

Start a film in your head. Let each thought be a frame. Move the frame very slowly until you're on the beach, resting in a lounge chair. Pick a special person to be with you, beside you. Feel what is happening to your body. Do you feel the warmth of the sun? Are the grains of sand hot against your feet? Can you smell the ocean? Can you hear the waves lapping against the beach? What is your companion doing? Are you happy? How does it feel? Move the frame forward very slowly. Now open your eyes. You're back in reality. Does your body change? In what way? The power of thought over our body is amazing. We can create feelings of cold as easily as feelings of warmth just by thinking about it.

Thoughts are so powerful that we have the power to create our future through thought. What will tomorrow, next year, or five years from now be like? We can determine it. Just think about it. Imagine it. We can have what we want. We need only to desire it and set a goal to attain it.

Sometimes we lose confidence and faith in our own judgment. I've learned that success in goal setting is dependent on trusting in that goal and in my own ability to achieve it; and trusting in a greater power that governs what happens to us. No matter what I set out to do, I use these two guides: desire and belief that my desire will come true.

Once we've expressed our desire, believe in it, and are confident that it will become a reality, we envision what it will look like. Visioning is a process used to assist us in understanding what our goals will look like. Companies use this process for goals to become real.

Meditating on one's desire is an ancient practice. Eastern philosophers and native peoples have long believed in the power of sending out one's thoughts beyond them. There's an aborigine tribe that can communicate telepathically to each other. They rarely need the spoken word. How can they do this and we can't? Or don't? They've learned that their own information and energy can interact through air and across distance.

Pat Riley, former coach of the Los Angeles Lakers, used visioning for his team to understand what they would be when they became a great team. Sports cybernetics, the concept that teaches sports figures to improve their skills through imagination and video taping, is all built on visioning. One must focus and meditate on the desire or goal. The skier must see herself skiing down the mountain through the powder. The manager must see herself as successful with her team. A lawyer must see herself as winning in the courtroom. You must see yourself as a happily married woman.

We understand how ideas, people, events, everything outside of us can affect us, but do we understand how we affect them with the signals we send, many of which we send subconsciously. Our thoughts, our feelings, our imagination, our beliefs, and our desires come alive because they're composed of information and energy. Your mother, sister, or best friend will know your feelings, your anger, joy, sickness, or happiness, without your saying a word. How? What's the signal you send? We send thoughts, desires, emotions, and instincts to people. How do they get received? They go out from us just as the air we breathe goes in and out of us and is picked up by receivers. Our bodies, our minds, our thoughts are not separate from that which is outside us. It's all information and energy being exchanged from one of us to the other in this universe.

Put your goal out there and focus on it. Your soul mate will pick up your energy. How will he do this? Something greater than you is directing your search. You will find that ordinary events in your life will become quite extraordinary. You will not be able to predict them but you can imagine them.

Imagine what your mate will look like. Envision the profile that you set. Remember your core values. List them one by one and see that person's behavior with these values. Picture your life after you marry this person. Let the process flow like a film in a movie. Move through the years. Picture participating in your favorite activities. If you want children, put them in your film. Visualize your mate as a parent. If you have children, visualize your mate as a stepparent.

Says Cindy about Cliff: "Everything that I imagined and hoped for, he was and still continues to be. From the very beginning he's been everything I wanted him to be towards me and towards my kids. He became the reality but I created him in my imagination."

Imagine the events that could be the circumstances for meeting your mate. Perhaps a friend will call you to go to the theater, or a coworker will invite you to go biking. Or you might be in the grocery store where you stopped off for some last-minute item. What are your interests? It could happen exactly as you imagine it or it might be a total surprise. Imagination is the beginning of making things happen. When you imagine, send out your message to your soul mate. Tell him that you're looking for him but that you're not going to do anything extraordinary so he needs to go where you're going.

Believe in your desires and goal. Some people who have taken our goal-setting training reacted to this plan with such enthusiasm that they forgot the basic premise that you must believe it will happen. You've set your goal. You've sent your message. Don't run around wildly looking for your mate. Do some things that present opportunities. But do them because you're interested, not because you're "looking."

Seek Opportunities

Just because you've envisioned him doesn't mean that he'll come to your door knocking. You've got to give him some help. Get involved in outside activities. Volunteer with a cause you're interested in. Make some effort to meet new friends.

Are you an Internet junkie? Try the love connections or personals or even the chat rooms for lawyers, doctors, computer programmers, real estate agents, accountants, executives, or a hundred others. Why not try a dating service or the personal ads? I know many women who have met a variety of interesting men through all of these means. Try all of these then carefully select those potential dates that fit your profile.

When you decide to meet one of these potential dates, meet in a safe place. Have lunch or meet after work in a public bar or restaurant. Don't go to his house or yours, or ride in a car alone with him, until you know a great deal about him. After the first phone call or the first meeting check him out with the information he gives you. Where does he work? In what activities is he involved? Find out as much as you can if you plan to see him again.

Sybil, a close friend of mine, dated a guy she met on the Internet for three months and he even asked her to marry him. One night at midnight her car broke down and she called his house for help. A woman answered and told her she had been living with this man for the past two months. Sybil had believed and trusted him without checking him out. On the other hand she's dated three or four men from the Internet who are top-notch people.

In addition to dating possibilities you may also meet some friends. Allison met on one of her sites a couple that she has known now for several years. The more doors you open the greater the chances for your soul mate to find you.

Consider the profile you set for your future mate. Does it suggest where that person may spend most of his time? Do you know anyone who can introduce you to an environment where you're likely to find your mate? When you look at the age range that you set, where do persons of that age frequent? Are singles clubs for you? Would you find someone in the bar scene? Are you a person who likes outdoor activity and are you looking for someone with those interests? Will you meet someone at the gym? Are you an artist or a photographer? Are you a hiker, a biker, or a mountain climber? Perhaps a class in any of these will help you to meet your mate. What about your goals of family orientation? Will your future partner be at the PTA?

List the activities you enjoy and people or places they may introduce you to.

Select from this list activities you haven't done in a while but that might take you down new roads for new experiences.

Fears and Excuses

You're undoubtedly asking at this point, What if I'm getting very close to my deadline and nothing has happened? This is the time when it's very important that you don't mistrust yourself, that you don't give up. If it's two months before your deadline, it's time to remind yourself to relax, your message has been sent. Continue to do your ordinary things. Go with life's flow. It's by not panicking that it will happen. Your future mate will be there. Trust.

My signals were picked up and I had to be fired to get me to go to Florida. Cliff and Cindy were definitely brought together by Cindy's sending out the message. Susan needed some help with a volunteer project and by chance found that help in Mark. Jessie and Paul met through someone with whom Jessie had shared her goal.

I hear from many women, especially those over the age of thirty-five, that there aren't any eligible men around. I hear from professional women: "There are just no men who want an independent, professional woman. They're afraid if I make more money than they do or if my job is more powerful." It isn't unusual to find some men who are threatened by competent women but intelligent, achieving women still turn on many men. And if there aren't eligible men in your profession or social circle it's time to expand your network.

I hear from the men here in the mountains of Colorado: "There are just not enough eligible good women." It's true that ski resort towns generally have more men than women. But the men are simply making excuses. Women skiers come from all over the country. These men travel, hike, raft, and bike. Women vacationers do all these things. If the men were serious, they would meet someone.

Cindy says, "I believe if there was only one man on an island and I was one of ten thousand women, I'd have that one man." That's the kind of confidence you must have in yourself.

Fear is often what keeps us from moving out and finding the mate of our desires and goals. We fear, therefore we create every excuse for why we haven't found a mate. We truly need to examine our own fears. Do we believe in ourselves enough to know that we can create a happy marriage? We're told that half the marriages in the United States end in divorce. When we look at that statistic, and maybe our place in that statistic, does it scare us? We might say that half the marriages in the United States don't end in divorce. We may even say great portions of these are happy marriages. Ask yourself why you couldn't be a part of this happy statistic.

For those of you who have come out of a first or even second marriage, perhaps you think love and life have eluded you. Perhaps you think that you've made poor decisions in the past. Perhaps you did. Haven't you also made some good ones? Focus on these good ones. Trust in your positive qualities. Trust in your ability to love and be loved. If you cannot convince yourself of your abilities to love and be loved, perhaps you may need to visit with a counselor who can encourage you to believe in yourself. Brenda did this and it helped change her life.

Whatever we pay attention to, give our energies to, gets accomplished. I'm sure you know from your work life that whatever you focus on gets done. What you don't focus on drops through the cracks. When we state a desire, we give it attention. This desire then becomes a goal. We give it the momentum to move toward whoever or whatever can help us achieve it. Commitment to the goal has the capability to transform and fulfill itself. Think positively and don't let fears get in the way.

We discussed how important it is to be detached from your goal in step two. It is good to think about this important element because trusting in Divine Providence or Fate or Universal Intelligence will help you to be detached. This act of trust will be tested often in your year of finding your soul mate. You will get uneasy when your deadline is approaching and you haven't met him. I find the people who do not trust in a power greater than themselves get easily discouraged and even appear obsessed with their goal. Remember, if you are obsessed you are not in control, you are not your best self. So trust in your soul mate, that he is looking for you, and in God, that She/He wants you to be happy.

In the next chapter we will start taking some external action. It's time to send out your message to those friends and family who can help you reach your goal.

STEP FIVE: GAIN SUPPORT
FOR YOUR GOAL

Tell Those Who Will
Support You

For many, this is the most embarrassing part of following. *The Marriage Plan.* Telling someone we want
to get married isn't usually something we shout from
the roof. In goal setting in business, it is important to
elicit the support of all the people who can help you
reach your goal. There are two reasons for this. First,
none of us can do anything alone. We need to interact with others to make sure that there are no obsta-
cles in our path to success; that others are not

working against us either consciously or unconsciously. Second, it keeps us strong in our determination. When we tell other people, we are affirming for ourselves that this is important to us and we are serious. Until we tell that first person, we'll not be sure that we believe it, and mean it.

Is there a conflict between making your goal public to your friends and remaining detached, trusting, and internally at peace with your goal? Some people tell us to keep our desires private lest people make fun of our efforts and weaken our determination. On the contrary, most people will support our goal if we're calm and serious about it. What's important is placing ourselves in situations and exploring opportunities where we can reach our goal.

Granted, it's very difficult for us to tell others, "I want to get married." Some of us will feel that we're revealing information that's too private. Getting married, however, is a very public act in that it's publicly recorded and published and legal. It's public in that it affects the families of both parties. Each family gets a new member. They have a right to know. So if the act of marriage is such a public event, why are we concerned that telling people we want to get married is too public?

Most of us feel that courtship is a private affair, yet we do our courting publicly. Stan and Laura worked at the same company within the same division. They tried to keep their relationship from workplace gossip and were successful for over six months. By the time they were "discovered," they had committed to each other and had decided to get married. Susan and Mark, who worked at the same company, also kept their courtship under wraps until they had set a wedding date. They had even moved in together and no one at work knew it. It was important for them to give their relationship a chance to mature before they became an item for public conversation.

We're seen together in public places. Sometimes we even show affection in public. Is it because courtship and being in love involves so much emotion that we want to keep these feelings private? Is it because we're afraid that we'll become the butt of gossip? Are we afraid that if the relationship doesn't work out, we'll be embarrassed and expected to answer many personal questions? No doubt all of these are present in our desire for privacy.

If you're a more private person than most people are, you may want to be highly selective with whom you share your goal. Sharing your goal with friends who can introduce you to potential partners is a good idea.

Tell a Friend Who Will Say,

"You Can Do It"

Throughout the goal-setting process I was fortunate to have a friend like Helen who kept saying, "You can do it." Cindy and Brenda were fortunate to have each other. They encouraged one another in their goals. Aimée was fortunate to have a dear friend in Hawaii, thousands of miles away, who by telephone encouraged her through the process. A very important step in any goal-setting process, but particularly in this plan, is to ask a friend who believes in you to be your support. It's good practice to share your desires with a friend of either gender who will continuously encourage you when you start to falter.

A true friend will not let you get discouraged; will not let you change your time frame even in the face of great crisis. Find this friend. Ask her or him to support you, because you'll need it through this process. If you're lucky to have more than one good friend who believes in you, all the better! Get as much support as possible.

A word about family! Be careful what you share with your family. They believe they have your best interests at heart and may not hesitate to deter you from your goal if they don't agree with it. Unless you have a family member who truly is a friend, and who supports you in all your undertakings, you may find that it doesn't help to involve family in this goal.

A counselor can be of significant encouragement in this process. Brenda's sessions helped her to understand the limitations she was putting on relationships as well as on herself. A counselor or therapist can help you work through your criteria, which is where you can mess up if you're confused about yourself. He or she can assist you to be honest in drawing up your mate's profile. You'll need encouragement. Use your friend, counselor, or supportive family member throughout your year of goal work.

You should now be ready to take some action steps. You've written out your statement and time frame: "I want to be married by _____ (no later than a year)." You've determined your core values; outlined the profile of the mate you would like to have; and sent out this desire and information in quiet meditation. You've listed the activities and places that will help you to get involved outside of your normal life. What will be your first action in the next twenty-four hours?

A good first step is to contact a friend and share your goal. Don't do it in the way that I did with my friend Roger. Prepare them. Talk about what is important to you and why you've made this decision. Tell them how important it will be for them to support you through this. If it's at all possible, try to do this in person rather than over the telephone, by e-mail, or in a letter. This isn't to say that these forms of communication wouldn't work. It's more helpful to have their full attention when you share this with them.

Make an effort to go over your full plan with your friend. Ask your friend to suggest some steps you might take in addition to the ones listed here. It's good to relate the whole plan to them because you'll hear yourself confirming your goal. You'll also listen to see if it makes sense to you now that you've had some time to think about it. If for some reason your friend doesn't support you, don't get discouraged. Have they supported you in your goals in the past? Do they love and care for you no matter what you do or have done? You'll find other support. Make this your first action step.

I'll tell _____ that I want to get married by _____ and want her/him to support me in this goal. I'll do this _____ (in person, by phone, by e-mail) tomorrow or by _____ (date).

In the next chapter we will discuss the importance of only dating people who fit your profile. If we violate this rule we will be wasting time and won't meet our goal within the year.

STEP SIX: DON'T DATE PARTIAL PROFILERS. FOCUS ON YOUR PROFILE

What is a partial profiler and why do we continue to date them and even keep long-term relationships going with them? A partial profiler is simply someone who does not match the characteristics that you need to make you happy. He may be a wonderful person, have great values, be likeable, a friend, passionate, great in bed, and a perfect match for someone else, maybe even one of your friends.

We need to be on guard against involving ourselves with partial profilers, either in a simple dating pattern or in an ongoing relationship. Partial profilers in either case can be very dangerous to our reaching our goal. The relationship with a partial profiler is usually powerful. This powerful attraction blinds us to reality. We rationalize and then we finally come to wisdom. He is not for us, and it is painful. Let's look at what happens to us in these situations.

Simple Dating

After you have set your profile, you need to keep it in focus at all times. Most will begin dating by meeting someone quite unexpectedly, through a chance meeting at an athletic event, a grocery store, a party, a bar, a concert, a volunteer event, a hobby or business conference, an airplane trip, or innumerable other circumstances. You may also meet quite expectedly through an introduction by a friend, searching the Internet or personal ads, or using a dating service. Whatever the circumstances, the plan will help us to exercise good judgment in accepting a second date. The first date will help us to determine whether our initial attraction is consistent with our core values. If this person is not a match, then there should be no second date. This rule saves time and effort and pain. You may argue, "I should give him a chance," or "How can I get to know someone from only one or two dates?" This is where trust comes in. You may have to fight loneliness, passion, a fun and interesting person, a friend's review of his great qualities, or an accusation that you're "too picky" to overcome the tendency to waste time on partial profilers. You can do it if you keep your profile in focus, trust in Divine Providence and in your soul mate who is looking for you.

Ongoing Relationship

Recently, a student of mine, Trisha, was telling me about her love relationship. She described her boyfriend, Shawn, as one whom she really loved. She was not living with him but they spent an enormous amount of time together and had a special connection. Their relationship was physical, fun, passionate, and open but often negative. They seemed to irritate each other very often to the point where they would argue quite strongly. It was depressing her. After some digging, I found out that Trisha really does want to get married and have children. Shawn is fairly certain he does want to get married but he does not want children. Intellectually she knew Shawn did not meet her profile. He did not accept her for who she was and was trying to change her. She did not want to change nor did she believe that she could. The things that irritated him were part of who she was. Yet she continued to date him even knowing that he was a partial profiler. Her emotions totally controlled her in this relationship.

Shawn did not share Trisha's core values: acceptance of who she is and having children. If they had developed a relationship of intimacy and knowledge about each other before they jumped into the sack, before they let passion and romance control their relationship, Trisha and Shawn would not be suffering the pain that they are today. They should have discussed core values in the very early stages of the relationship and they both would have known that they were partial profilers for each other. She finally broke off the relationship but is enduring great trauma over the separation. It will take her some time to recover before she can let her soul mate into her life. Although it was a growth experience for her, she wasted precious time, as did he.

So many of us repeat the Tricia-Shawn relationship. It is classic. We fall in lust, and even maybe in love, and then we find out that there is no match on the things we hold as core to our souls. Yet we continue in the relationship with a partial profiler because we believe that he will change. This is usually based on false hope. It's painful to break off a relationship with a partial profiler because he has so many external qualities that seem to fulfill our needs. He's not a "no profiler." If he were, it would be easy to break the relationship. He has attractive characteristics but he lacks the shared core values. He's a partial profiler.

Even sometimes when we know intellectually and emotionally that he won't change, we keep dating someone because it's comfortable or because we are fearful of being alone. We often choose this partial profiler to overcome loneliness, our need for sexual satisfaction, or to build our low self-esteem. These are not reasons to select a lifetime partner. We need to find ways to deal with each of these without compromising our goals and our deadline. The program *Sex and the City* on HBO television illustrates our point. Four thirty-something women seem to date for all these reasons, yet they know that the people they are dating are partial profilers, some even no profilers. The more they date these characters, the more their self-esteem decreases. The main character seems to be the most hooked in an ongoing relationship with "Mr. Big." He treats her like a yo-yo, doesn't show up for dates, keeps telling her that he isn't interested in commitment, but she seems to be eternally hoping he will change because she is definitely hooked on lust and passion. Sometimes she'll show signs of being in control by confronting him but he knows, and she knows, that she has not yet made a permanent decision to drop him. Does this sound familiar to you? The television program is successful because it imitates life.

Most of us have been in such a relationship, hooked on passion, lust, good looks, great sex, the power and status of our boyfriend, the places he takes us, the people we mingle with, the excitement of a faraway weekend, even the friendship of a member of his family. But most frequently we are hooked on the fear of being lonely, the fear of confronting ourselves as a full human being who is capable of loving herself, entertaining herself, and developing into an independent, in-control woman. It is when we work on our own interests, our own values, giving to others instead of worrying about ourselves that we'll have the courage to drop the partial profiler and move on to find our soul mate.

If you find you are feeling sorry for yourself, if you find you are lonely, if you find that all of your thoughts are about you, then perhaps you are not ready to find your soul mate and have some work to do. Try getting out of the house. Do things with your friends, develop new interests, volunteer to help those in greater need than you, read, direct your interests beyond your self-centeredness. When you do, you'll find this lack of self-centeredness will make you attractive to your soul mate. Remember that the most important person in the world to you is you. Love yourself as you deserve to be loved, as a full human being who is not self-centered, who is ready to meet her soul mate. You have only one life to live (that we know of). Make it the best you can. Don't waste time on people who do not have what it takes to give you what you need to be happy. Don't date partial profilers.

In the next chapter we'll address the importance of not playing games with your potential partner. This openness is a time-saver and a call to value your self.

STEP SEVEN: BE OPEN
AND DIRECT. DON'T
PLAY GAMES

Don't Play Games

What are games? Games in a dating relationship are deliberate deceit or hiding of who we truly are out of fear the other person won't accept us as valuable. The most common game people play in dating is "hard to get." "I'm not going to let you know how interested I am because you may think I'm easy, or even not very attractive to other people." This game means lying about being available when the dating partner wants to date you more frequently. It means that you don't tell him how you feel about him or anything else until you're sure that he is more than

just a casual relationship. These "old game tapes" are for high
school and college dating. They are not for people over the age of
twenty-five who are interested in finding a soul mate.

Paul and Jessie started out on a very engaging first date. Paul
had been engaged previously and had several long-term meaningful relationships and he had set a goal to get married. He knew
what he wanted. Jessie had an excellent career but she was unhappy with her personal life. She thought perhaps she'd meet
someone she could marry if she transferred to the company's
Boston operation. She tells us:

Wheatly was a small community and I didn't think I'd find
anyone I could spend my life with here. I knew a lot of
people in larger communities that hadn't found a partner
either. I only needed one man but where was he? I wanted
someone who was more liberal and more supportive of
feminist behavior than my former husband.

I met Paul shortly after I put in for the transfer. Some
friends asked me to go to a party with them and told me
they wanted me to meet this man. I had very low expectations but I talked to him at the party. When we were ready
to leave, Paul asked, "Can I call you?" I said, "Sure," and
headed out. He came running after me and said, "But I
don't have any information to call you." So I gave him a
check stub with my phone number printed on it. "Here,
this is all you'll need. You can put money in it or you can
call me at this phone number."

He called me right after that and invited me to dinner.
Basically he interviewed me during dinner. He asked me
all these questions. "Do you smoke? What do you like to
do? What's your religion?" It was like going right down a

checklist. Finally at the end I said, "Are you interviewing here?" He turned red and said, "Well yeah, I guess I am. There are some things I'm interested in knowing before we ever go any further." This was our first real date.

I had several broad parameters for the man I was going to marry but nothing that made me ask the same kind of questions. I wanted somebody who was working and seemed to have a good livelihood and was financially solvent. I wanted children but I wanted to work after I had children. That had to be real clear.

Both Paul and Jessie knew they wanted to be married and they started out from the very beginning with honest conversation. Paul took the lead and Jessie was quite surprised but she understood very early what Paul wanted. She also did not hesitate to tell him what was important to her. There would be no games in this relationship. This may seem like heavy conversation for a first date and perhaps many people would be frightened by the direction of the conversation. For people who know what they want, however, it is not intimidating.

A student in one of my seminars on the East Coast told us a story about a man she had been dating two or three times a week for three months. He told her he was going away for a week to Colorado on a business trip and couldn't call her. This was a trip to Denver, not to the backwoods. Some members of the class reminded her that they have telephones in Denver and that even cell phones work there. He was definitely playing a game with her. Was he visiting another woman? Was there something he was trying to hide? It appeared that the relationship had not deepened in those three months. She felt that the distancing he sometimes produced in the relationship was the way he was. He was fearful of getting too close but she felt time would heal this. She was definitely being fooled and being a fool. She was not looking out for her own welfare and was giving him permission to play games with her. Sometimes he would call her before these dates and sometimes he would just show up at her door. And sometimes he would call her and not show up. She tolerated this behavior and he continued to treat her this way until suddenly the Denver episode tripped her switch and the light went on. She was involved in a relationship that was going nowhere.

The games people play with our hearts have no place in a dating relationship that is directed toward deepening the desires of two souls for each other. I like to make a distinction between dating and developing a relationship. Dating is for practice. It helps us to grow and to learn about relationships. Sometimes it's for pure fun. It often does have games involved which are not healthy for either party. It's for people who are not serious about finding a permanent partner at this certain point in their lives. When one sets a goal to get married, one is serious about developing a relationship. Trust, honesty, and integrity characterize the relationship. This not only enables the couple to get to know each other at a faster pace than normal but it also lays a solid foundation for a soul mate marriage.

Put a premium on honesty, integrity, and openness with yourself and with your potential mate. Often when we fall in lust, the relationship starts out with submissiveness, compliance, and awe. As we continue dating, reality sets in and we have a serious disagreement. We're filled with frustration, dissatisfaction, and anger. To soothe things over, we practice indirect manipulative games. We're not true to ourselves and to what we want. Our relationship then has a rocky foundation.

If you want a stable marriage, base it on a solid foundation.

Don't play games with your potential mate and don't allow him to play games with you. People who use dishonesty, lies, stories, and bragging are off to a deadly start in a relationship. Return phone calls if you want to continue the relationship. Don't say you're busy, when you're not, just to keep him on a string. Be direct with him in what you want. Don't play "Indirect Irene" and hope he guesses what he did wrong. Don't be "Helen Hinter" and hope he picks up the hints of what you want, where you want to go, or what movie you want to see. Don't agree with him on issues just to please him. If you disagree, be direct. He must know you as you are. Don't pretend to be something you're not. Such deception cannot last. Game playing definitely doesn't establish stable relationships.

Be self-confident if you want to find your soul mate. Believe in yourself and you'll come to your soul mate with self-respect. That's how you'll get him to respect you. As a person in control of your life, set out to get what you want without destroying either your own or your mate's self-esteem. Self-confidence helps us to set goals and to believe in our ability to reach them. Setting goals and going after them also reinforces our self-confidence.

This book is for you who have come to terms with your own needs and are not afraid to declare them. This doesn't mean that you've resolved all your problems. It does mean that you're working on a healthy self-concept, which implies you accept responsibility for who you are and see yourself as worthy of respect and love. When two people bring healthy self-concepts to a marriage they've brought a tremendous dowry. Each individual comes to the marriage with a vision and goals that assure that one's individuality will not be lost.

You want passion and sex, sensuousness and excitement. During those moments of mundane living, washing dishes, doing laundry, shopping for groceries, or treating a headache, you need and want him most. He must be there when your children are facing a crisis or a parent is dying.

These inner strengths of self-confidence and belief in each other, the passion of love, the sensuousness and excitement of life, our fantasies, and our desires feed the soul. Did your past loves, lusts, or affairs feed your soul? Follow this plan and it will help you to attract your mate. He *will* come. You *can* have him. He's there waiting for you but remember that you control his entrance into your life.

Many people question the value of marriage. Recently my friend Renée, said to me, "Why is marriage necessary? If I have this special relationship, why do I need this piece of paper? I don't see any value to it and it can screw up a good thing." Another friend, Maura, found her friend but believes marriage would only complicate their financial status. She and her friend have a good deal of money and she sees only legal entanglements.

I'm not advising marriage to those who don't want it. Don't get married if you don't see its value. If you don't believe in marriage's sacred bond, then don't enter into it. Marriage is more than signing a contract. It's a holy passage of two lives into one life, a sacred trust in one's self and in each other. You'll care, respect, and love not only when it's fun, but also when it's hard. Only then will you know you are soul mates.

STEP EIGHT: TELL HIM
YOUR GOAL

Tell Your Potential Mate

You must tell your potential mate what your intentions are. All the goal setters among these couples say this is very difficult. We're not used to being this direct with our potential mate in the beginning of a relationship. We feel weird doing this. Sometimes we're afraid he'll get frightened and go running. Sometimes we feel that it's just inappropriate.

Granted, there are many steps in this plan that won't be in keeping with the traditional ways of dating; nevertheless it's important to tell him early if you're serious about your goal. You're trying to eliminate the poor match. It's exactly what we *have* to do. If he's not ready to marry in your time frame, he's not your soul mate.

Oh no! Do I have to tell him about my goal as soon as you and Cindy did? Well, you do have to do it early in the relationship. How early depends on when you get *emotionally hooked* into this man. Do it before you get painfully hurt if he eventually walks away. This is one of the principal reasons that I recommend strongly that there be no sexual intercourse before commitment. When you're beginning to fall in love is the time to tell your mate what you want out of your relationship. When you want to have sex in order to make love, and not just for physical gratification, it's time to announce that your goal is to get married.

It's time to gather your strength and be confident and comfortable. You want to be sure he understands that you simply want him to know what you want and are not trying to pressure him in any way. Be open to his feelings but don't let him discourage you from being forthright. You want to find out where he is because there's no point in becoming more involved if you have different goals.

The most comfortable situation is one that arises naturally. You may be discussing someone else's getting married, or you've been to a movie about romance and marriage, or you've read an article that seems comfortable to discuss. These can be easy segues into telling him about your desires and your goal.

Telling your potential mate that you want to get married and within a reasonable time frame will definitely clear the air. It will let him know that you're taking this relationship seriously and if he isn't, you'll know. Although it may be temporarily painful, it's best that you know. Don't construct a scenario in which you convince yourself that he'll change his mind. This will waste good years of your life. This may sound callous, but you must be willing to accept that he might bolt. If you get the feeling that he is not where you are, it will take all the courage you can muster to let him go. In being up front and direct with your potential mate you won't waste time or energy with someone who has other goals. How else will you know whether this is your soul mate unless you let the person know you're very clear that you want to get married?

Be Up Front

Not only must you tell your mate your goal but you also must be up front with him about the most important things going on in your life. He must get to know you with all of your strengths and frailties. He must get to know your family issues, your deepest desires, hopes, dreams, and fears. Without this directness your chances of wasting time and emotional energy are quite high. Remember the pain you had in other relationships at break up time? The longer you're in a relationship, the more pain there is in ending it.

Make sure he knows all the important information about you. If he cannot accept this openness, then that's a sure sign that he cannot accept you as you are. Deciding what information is necessary for your potential mate to have is important. Most people agree that you should not share your past liaisons or sexual experiences unless it affects the other's physical health in some way.

You'll also want to know his deepest desires, hopes, fears, family issues, and previous difficulties he may have had in relationships. You'll hope that he will offer this information when you offer yours but if he doesn't, you must ask. If you find he is closed to you and you feel your relationship should be deepening, then you have a warning sign about his being your soul mate.

If you discover something about him that you feel would be a real obstacle to a happy marriage, it's time for you to break off the relationship. Don't live with the false hopes that he will change. Accept that this person isn't for you. Move on. If you bought this book because you want to get married, and you've followed everything in it up to this point, then continue to believe in yourself, no matter how painful the termination of the relationship might be.

The next chapter directs you toward the critical soul communication between mates, developing intimacy and friendship. You will learn how to do this quickly and in depth and how to determine whether the person who received your signal is your soul mate.

STEP NINE: DEVELOP INTIMACY

Intimacy

Most people confuse intimacy with sex but the two are very different. *Webster's Third New International Dictionary* defines intimate as "relating to an inner character or essential nature; the innermost true self; characteristic of the genuine core of something."

Intimacy, the sharing of your true self, is what you search for in a relationship. Recognizing this desire for intimacy in a potential mate will tell you that he's your soul mate. Most of us are sick of pretending to be something we're not, of having to put on a show for the sake of being attractive to someone.

When we have intimacy, the other accepts us for who we are. He doesn't require our face to be made up all of the time but he appreciates it when it is. He respects and loves our naturalness.

Telling someone how you feel without being ashamed of the way you feel is the comfort you seek in an intimate relationship. Intimacy is being able to talk about your deepest feelings toward your family, about your sex life, your friends, and your job and having him be supportive and accepting. You know he won't gossip to his friends about what you say about your friends or parents. He holds the relationship sacred. You trust him to do this and there are never any questions about his breaking the trust.

You'll trust the mate that you've found not to talk about your sex life to his buddies. You know that he values and protects the intimacy you've created. Both of you willingly open yourselves to each other and take your love to a deeper level of sharing based on this trust.

The kind of partnership desired in a marriage is one in which both people want and work toward this intimacy. You can have the closeness, exclusivity, depth of understanding, and exchange of feelings that the couples in this book achieved. Each of the mates had this feeling of oneness as his or her prime objective in their search for a partner.

There's a difference between having an exclusive relationship with your mate and expecting him to be everything to you. You both need to have your own identities and individual lives. You don't give up your identity when you get married. You're two individuals who will come together because you want to be with each other. You'll need your other friends and interests. You would soon dry up and become bored with each other if you had no interests outside of the marriage.

Courtship is the time when you spend almost all your time

with your newfound love. You'll be so entranced and caught up with each other that you'll devote every waking moment to each other. This changes as time goes on. As you begin to trust and know the other person, you'll feel comfortable being yourselves, having your interests, and sharing him with your family and friends. If you have hobbies, you'll need to get back to them. If it's true for you, it's also true for your mate. He too needs to get back to his individual interests. When you reach this stage it will add to your relationship and intimacy. It should not interfere with it.

Often intimacy is developed after a common critical happening, joyous or tragic. True friendships are bonded because people share deep emotions. More often it occurs under more mundane circumstances, because two people are eager and willing to share their feelings.

Getting married within seven weeks of meeting is highly unusual. It was possible for Robert and me because we talked for sometimes eight hours or more at a time, day in and day out, or rather night in and night out. We shared everything that we needed to. We had a respect for each other's past and allowed the other to talk about what he or she wished. Rarely did either of us feel excluded from the other's important feelings or understandings. If we did, then we would ask the questions that needed answers to make us feel comfortable.

Brenda saw Johnny's openness and directness as a willingness to be secure in his own vulnerability, and therefore secure enough to accept hers.

From the first night, I talked to him every single day. It terrified me after about the third week. "This is not good. I like him," I told my friend Betty. "I don't need this." I was getting hooked emotionally because I'd never met a man so honest. What attracted me to him was his openness. We would talk all night and then get up and go to work at five o'clock. No sex, we were just talking. I thought that it was great but it was also a little strange.

I could always say what I wanted and he could too. He'd tell me how he saw me as a person. People don't usually do that but we did. We were always honest. Honesty for me was important. I guess it was because so many other people were deceptive.

I remember telling him the night we first had sex that "I think this is going to change everything." He said, "Yeah," very slowly. Well things only got better.

A strong successful marriage is two healthy "I's" coming together as "We." It's important that the "I's" retain their individual identities to grow into a "We." The presence of both supports the intimacy of a happy marriage. Intimacy is about equality and mutual respect in a relationship. This is essentially dependent on retaining the "I." Intimacy is also about the exclusivity, the special sharing that occurs because the relationship has become an entity in itself, a "We." It's this special sharing that you want to look for in a courtship. If it's not present in a courtship, it's rare for it to be present later.

All of our women identified the signs of their mates' willingness to be intimate. The signs were common:

❀ He wanted to spend hours talking about all kinds of things.
❀ He talked about his feelings and was sensitive to her feelings.

❀ He was willing to share the intimate details of his life.

❀ He demonstrated a love that was unselfish, going the extra mile to be kind and caring with her.

❀ He was openly affectionate, warm, and kind. There were lots of "I love you's," kisses, and hugs. Physical contact was always welcome.

Four things are necessary for intimacy: the depth and frequency of valuable verbal communication; closeness; exclusive sharing of secret thoughts and feelings; and mutual love and respect.

The couples achieved intimacy because early in the dating stage the person setting the goal expected intimacy and got it. In almost all cases both partners wanted marriage for companionship, to belong, to share a life together, for closeness.

Many couples have marriages of long duration, thirty, forty, or even fifty years, but never have a relationship of any intimacy. They've stayed together and may have come to mutual acceptance of their state. Most of us don't want to have that kind of marriage. We want warmth, love, acceptance, trust, companionship, support, and the intimacy these values create.

Males and Intimacy

Michael McGill reported in his study on male intimacy that hundreds of couples said their marriages lacked intimacy. Many men saw intimacy as a liability, as something that made them vulnerable. They had no desire to share information about themselves, their feelings, their careers, or any part of their work or play lives with their wives. Many wives in McGill's study complained that their husbands did not know them or their children. Many husbands felt their wives judged their marriage and his behavior based on her needs not on his. Clearly most of these people hadn't found their soul mates.

He found men fear that their wives want their husbands to be dependent on them. One husband expressed his need for emotional independence: "I don't think any of us should get dependent on anyone else because when it comes down to it, you can't depend on anyone but yourself." Another said, "If my wife was my lover, my best friend, my companion, my partner in everything, the way she'd like to be, and she left me, then where would I be? This way if she leaves me, all I've lost is a wife." Neither of these men developed the kind of trust in their wives that's characteristic of soul mates. They misjudged what their wives wanted. The women wanted their marriage to be special, exclusive. They didn't expect nor want to be all things to their husband. McGill believes that men confuse exclusivity, a key ingredient for intimacy, with all-inclusive.

McGill claims that in most marriages women are the ones who want intimacy because they're romantic while men seek more reality. He learned that in most cases, the men were also seeking closeness but not with their wives, and not necessarily in an affair. The husband would have a close woman friend, a sister, or even his mother in whom he confided. He sought closeness but not at the risk of losing his independence. In most of these relationships with other women such a risk was minimal. With his wife, he believed that his openness would risk his marriage. Often the lack of sharing had just the opposite effect of what he intended. It often led to divorce.

Unlike the males in McGill's report, the males in this book sought closeness with their life partners and tested that out before they were married. For them, as for the women, intimacy *was* the reality. Romance came later. Intimacy came through voluntarily revealing their personal selves. Closeness came about through expressions and behavior that demonstrated caring and concern, through the true giving of oneself not only to the potential partner but also to others, and through the frequency of meaningful communication.

Johnny did not fall in love with Brenda immediately, far from it.

> When I first met Brenda I told her about everything in my life. I went into great detail about my sick alcoholic life and she still wanted to be my friend. I was the kind of individual that she should have run away from.
>
> I didn't discover I was "in love" with Brenda until two years into the marriage. I've always admired her, I'm always learning from her, but I never knew what love was. I didn't love myself; how could I give her any love? It's been growing ever since and now I couldn't live without her.

Although Johnny didn't realize he was "in love" with Brenda until two years into the marriage, they did develop intimacy before marriage. Each of them cared for the other when they were ill. They told each other secrets and they were exclusive in their relationship.

For Don the women he dated needed to demonstrate an ability to be intimate. He and Aimée had this kind of relationship. Yet he was concerned about their relationship because he had no "in love" feelings for her, the opposite extreme of his past relationships.

I liked Aimée as a person more and more and wanted to be her friend. I grew to love her as a friend as I did my other friends. Yet I was concerned that I wasn't falling in love with her; she did not hook me like other women had.

My men's group told me to be patient, that it would happen. This is the first relationship in which I went through the stages of becoming an acquaintance, then becoming friends, and becoming a lover at the end rather than the other way around.

While we were dating, Aimée and I spent lots of intimate time together without getting involved sexually. We packed up our horses and went into the wilderness. We got to know each other and got along beautifully. I knew from Aimée's energy that she wanted a deeper commitment, possibly even marriage. Although she didn't say this, I could feel it emanating from her. I believed she had an agenda about this relationship.

Paul also valued the warmth and romance of their relationship. He, from the very beginning, broke through any walls by asking Jessie very direct questions.

The very first weekend we went to dinner, I asked Jessie what her dreams were. I was interested in knowing what she saw as her future. At that point anything about her, and what her hopes were, was very interesting to me.

I was looking for companionship. Jessie is the kind of person that I want to be with. I have a lot of shortcomings and I'm quite willing these days to admit that. Yet she's been there for me, given me my chance to be myself, for better or for worse, and I think it has made me better. I realize that a relationship is hard work. And I make it hard work for her sometimes.

Cliff fell easily into an intimate relationship with Cindy.

I fell in love with Cindy probably the first time I saw her. It took me two weeks to get the nerve up to call her for a date. She accepted (to my surprise) and from that night we dated at least ninety days in a row. I was working hard every day so sometimes I'd go to work to rest so that I could go out that night. We became very close in that period of time.

The more I got to know Cindy, the more I knew that the bad things that I had experienced in the past weren't going to be in this marriage.

When you're dating and looking for a life mate, determine the other's openness to intimacy. He must be immediately willing to go to that deeper level if he's the right mate for you. It must be an emotional partnership.

Emotional Partnerships

All of the marriages of our couples are emotional partnerships. As Jessie says, "It's not a business partnership; it's not a financial partnership. It's an emotional partnership." Both mates must invest their emotions in the relationship from the beginning. Intimacy depends on the expression of feelings and emotions. When they are expressed honestly and accepted without judgment, the foundation for the emotional partnership is laid.

TRUST

One partner cannot be open, trustful, and truthful while the other is closed, distrustful, or a liar. Cindy found out very early in the relationship that Cliff was the kind of man to be trusted.

> Cliff was kind, even a little vulnerable. He didn't seem cocky or anything like that; he was humble and that attracted me. I had learned to trust him. I think when you don't go to bed with a person and you get a chance to talk about your hopes, your fears, your aspirations, and your past, you're able to go to a deeper level of trust. Men don't often bother to go to that deeper level when you jump in the sack with them. All we did was talk about ourselves and how we feel.
>
> I had no question that he wanted to get married even though he said he'd never marry again. I think the difference was talking about commitment and connecting with him at a level that he wanted.
>
> Certainly you're going to have to like each other. You can't just walk up to somebody and say, "I want a commitment." With Cliff it was a love feeling. With Jim (the guy I broke my engagement with), it was [only] a respect feeling. This difference made me realize I wanted Cliff.

Johnny found in Brenda the first person he could ever trust and who trusted him.

> I trusted Brenda and I've never trusted anybody else. If she said she was going to do something she did it. I've never

caught her in a lie. I haven't lied to her but she says that I "add yeast" to stories. If there's an event, I dress it up a bit to make it more interesting.

"Can one tell little white lies?" is a question I'm often asked. One cannot do anything that betrays trust. If your partner can't believe what you say, or is unsure of your stories, then the foundation for trust crumbles. For a marriage to be intimate and fulfilling, trust must always be present. If you can develop trust with your potential mate in a short period of time, certainly after several months, then you can lay a strong foundation for a fulfilling marriage. If you can't, move on.

FEELING POWERFUL

Emotional partnerships also require that both people feel powerful because they feel equal.

It (our relationship) is equal. I feel I can influence her more at any given time than she can influence me. Sometimes I think I deliberately let her influence me. I'm sure that she'd say the same thing. I think we both have a lot of power in the marriage and neither of us feels powerless.

Feeling that you are able to influence or be influenced gives one confidence. Note that Cliff says that "at any given time," he feels powerful and at other times Cindy will feel powerful. Control or domination is shared.

Sharing power or dominance doesn't mean that he must believe as you do or take your disagreement in stride. It means that he may fight with you, raise his voice, slam the door, or temporarily walk away. It means above all that he'll return to love you more because he believes in you and respects you. You'll know that he can trust your anger and you can trust his. Getting angry isn't fatal; it can be used to help us grow. Anger and disagreement testify to our individuality and help us to establish bounds of who we are with the other.

Not everyone gets angry and confronts. Many people feel their marriage is strong because they have learned to walk away. The results of not confronting may be resentment or it may be that some people simply feel it's not worth the effort and they are fine with their nonconfrontational style. They choose to pick their battles. Or they know the issue is not important enough to argue about. In every relationship there will be times when each partner will need to let things go or let something slide. They do not feel less powerful because they do not confront. Feeling powerful depends on who you are and whether you are at peace with your style of interaction.

In courtship as in marriage, look closely at your and your mate's patterns of domination. Do you take turns at being in control? More importantly, is control balanced between you?

FUN AND PLAY

Emotional partnerships include lots of fun and play. Paul brought Jessie closer to him through play.

The same things that attracted me to Paul still attract me. He's a nice guy who likes to do a lot of things. He likes to sail, to snow ski, to play trombone, which I don't play but can appreciate. He was always on the road, always on the go doing something and that was good. I needed to learn a lot about how to have fun; he knew a lot about it.

I've learned how to have fun: sail, ski, and travel to many different places. I've learned how to have a child with somebody who is a pretty free spirit. They used to call him Breezy in his college fraternity. He still has the free spirit but he probably doesn't think so. He thinks he has a lot of responsibility because of the kids, and he does, though he still likes to say, "Let's do something fun. All work and no play makes you dull, Jessie." If it weren't for Paul, I'd be more of a crotchety old lady in a not-so-old body.

Cindy says, "We had lots of fun, we laughed, danced, and enjoyed each other in many ways. Even today we spend Sunday afternoon having fun. It's important to us."

Cliff says Cindy is still fun.

She always does something spectacular that enhances my life. She's more of a giver than a taker. Whenever I go to the racetrack, I'll give her a hundred-dollar bill. She'll say, "Cliff, you don't have to do that."

"Don't worry about that hundred-dollar bill," I say. "I'm going to get five hundred dollars back." I always get from her much more than I give in laughter, in hugs, in love, and in dollars.

Laura and Stan spend time traveling in their motor home. From the beginning of their courtship they would take weekends in the mountains of Canada or exploring Toronto. Don and

Aimée love to go horseback riding and camping. Robert and I love fairs and parks, going on rides, and eating hot dogs and cotton candy. Learning to play like children is part of the joy of courtship. Telling funny stories, acting like clowns, sharing humorous happenings with just a glance is exciting and brings us to a deeper level of love.

How Do You Speak
to Each Other?

COMMUNICATION AND INTIMACY

Communication ranges along a continuum with four specific points: public, private, personal, and intimate. It's this fourth point, intimate, that couples seeking their soul mates will set out to achieve from the moment she or he sets the goals and profile.

You can measure where in this range your potential partner might fall. Is he willing to share personal hopes, fears, fantasies, and dreams with you? Where do you fall? Are you willing to move from the discussion of general, public topics to intimacy very quickly? Public topics put a safe distance between people. It takes no courage or care to discuss a local or national issue or the last game of the Chicago Bulls. Private communication, such as where you live, what kind of work you do, where you went to school, or whether you have children, is usually cocktail talk so that people may become more comfortable with each other. Personal information, such as the amount of the mortgage payment or your salary, your family illnesses, or any general gossip about friends and coworkers, is usually only shared among good friends.

Your sex life, your fears, problems, hopes, and dreams are the intimate topics only for those very trustworthy and closest family and friends. These intimacies make us vulnerable and we must feel secure before we share them.

DIRECTNESS

We're sometimes timid to be open and direct with those who are closest to us. We fear that they won't respect us; that they may even turn against us. We're not confident in being who we are. If we want to form a deep relationship with our lifetime partner, we must learn to practice being direct and open without fear.

Women and men often communicate differently. It's helpful to understand some common differences so that we allow each other the freedom to be who we are.

We women, in general, learn to be nurturing from the earliest moments of our lives. By the age of two we've learned to identify with our nurturing mothers. We're taught to give, to care, and we do. It's also expected of us. Affection, association, and belonging are high on our scale of needs. In order to achieve this belonging, we give and often don't know when to stop. As adults, many of us women give too much, especially when dating. When that happens, our partner rejects us, feeling he's suffocating and must get away from the relationship in order to breathe emotionally and psychologically. Remember to let your partner breathe.

I've watched my dear friends, my daughters, my students, myself, give in our relationships with men until we saw ourselves behave like fools. Melissa, a college student, was involved with Brian, another college student. He felt smothered and ran. He wouldn't talk to her. To get some results she went to the extreme.

She called his mother and let her know what she thought of her son. His mother, although sympathetic, didn't know the circumstances and didn't believe Melissa. Her call brought no results; Brian never even bothered to acknowledge it. Melissa only felt guilty about her behavior, which reinforced her own poor self-image.

When Pete stopped calling Jane every night and began to put longer and longer intervals between their dates, Jane would call Pete. Sometimes she'd call him at work several times a day. During these calls she'd repeatedly ask what she was doing wrong. What was it about her that he didn't like anymore? Pete was suffocating and every time she called, it was becoming more and more difficult for him to breathe in the relationship. He broke away without telling her why.

In both these instances we find that the woman gave beyond her mate's limits to accept. The men only wanted time to process the relationship. By bugging him, both Melissa and Jane drove the male partner further away. It could be that during the process he'd have pulled away anyway. He may, however, have communicated more directly about their relationship if he was left alone. A relationship will not be nurtured if one is smothered.

It's also difficult for men to be direct in personal relationships. Normally none of us like to confront the disagreeable. Don, however, is the exception to this norm. When he calmly invited Aimée to his home, he took a few moments to write down some examples of how critical she was of him during the evening. He wasn't angry but he thought it was important for him to let her know if they were to continue the relationship. She had to know what she was doing to him and that he wouldn't tolerate it. He didn't use those words but they had the same effect on Aimée. She understood and loved him for it. It enabled both of them to move off the personal and politeness stage of the relationship very early and move to intimacy.

The tendency of both men and women to keep their relationship on that superficial, polite level makes intimacy so difficult in courtship and in marriage. It's important to practice intimacy and to embrace it.

Many men are fearful of hurting the woman's feelings, and of triggering a blow up, either their partner's or their own. They often don't know how to deal with women's emotions. We're all familiar with the effect crying women have on many men. Whether it's in the courtship, marriage, or workplace, emotional women often scare men, who then run away. On the other hand men who blow off steam often frighten women. If both genders would consider the other's emotions objectively and try to stand in the other's shoes, then the emotions would not be a barrier to communication.

If both partners would practice being direct, no matter what the emotion, the way Don did, then the disagreements wouldn't have to be so frightening to either. Don could have been fearful of Aimée's running away. He wasn't. If she had, he'd have had to accept that. She could have gotten defensive and angry. She didn't. She became embarrassed that she had been so insensitive and apologized. Their story is an excellent model for us in our interactions with our mates.

We also have the right to determine how much space we want to give to our mate. If caveman behavior is his need and his normal way of reacting to stress, we can set limits on how much we can take. Suppose he needs to be alone more than you can be comfortable with, what do you do? Try to expand your comfort level and give him his alone time for a short while. Sometimes our limits need to be broadened. We can take up a hobby that interests us while giving him his time. At the same time you may want to examine why you feel you have to be included in all that he does. Are you overreacting? Could you give him more space?

Request what time you need to be together. Explore what satisfies both of you. Listen to what he tells you, and tell him the honest truth. If this doesn't work, then it's best to remember that some men never grow up, never move past the fraternity years of college, the beer-drinking-after-work or every-night-of-the-week sports stage. If your potential mate is one of these, then he's not ready for marriage. You'll be playing second fiddle to the boys every night. The relationship demanded for a successful marriage is one where you're first in his affections, demonstrated by the time that he wants to spend with you and the time you need. If he can't give this to you, then it's best that you move on.

Self-confident communication is based on a solid self-concept. It means I know what my basic needs are, what I want. I ask for them and I expect it. Don't express doormat, passive behavior. Reject thoughts like "I don't want to hurt him"; "Maybe he needs more time"; "I don't want to lose him"; "I'm afraid he'll think I'm pushing him"; or "I want to support him"; "The poor man, he has so many problems to work out." These are not your problems; they're his. Don't make them yours. They're self-destructive and could turn you into a doormat on which he'll wipe his boots as he turns around to leave you. You're not responsible for his reactions or problems. You *are* responsible for fulfilling your goals. If he's the one for you, then his response will be what you need. If he's not, his response will leave you frustrated, unsatisfied.

We waste too much time foolishly blaming ourselves for the mate's problems. Don't stop setting limits because he has different motivations or problems. If he loves you, he'll find a way to solve his problems.

Cindy tells us how she tries to be direct with Cliff and how important it is in their marriage:

> I communicate with him directly. He may not agree but I do. He'll talk about it a little bit but he'll go underground. One day when we're out having dinner or we're here down in the steam room or something like that, he'll tell me that he knows that he behaved in a way that doesn't make sense and he's not going to do that again. That's when I know that we're taking another step in terms of our communication. But it takes him a long time. I usually don't let something go two days. I'll tell him as soon as I spot it. I don't like to be uncomfortable with him. I try to make it right between us very quickly.
>
> We tell each other what we like about each other much more than we tell what we don't like. It's so reinforcing it's unbelievable. The more we say it the more it's so.

When the results of your passive behavior become frustrating to you, and your mate is not moving toward marriage, you'll often be tempted to be indirect, manipulative, only hinting at what you want. Soon you'll discover that this behavior doesn't work.

If you do these things, you've forgotten the two most important aspects of *The Marriage Plan:* one, believing that the right person for you will receive your message; two, being direct about your goals. If he's not willing to work with you, then you must move on. Your future spouse will come of his own free will. If he's manipulated, the relationship will be short-lived. Above all, you must be in control.

Most of our mothers and grandmothers, along with many

women of their generations, were trained in manipulation. Until recently most women couldn't achieve public or personal power without manipulation. It was the commonly accepted tactic among women. They would set themselves up as helpless creatures who needed protection and care, all the while setting up the male to get what they want. The male who gives in later feels conned and then mistrusts the woman's future motivations.

If you begin to manipulate during your courtship period, your marriage will not be one of equality. You'll be constantly involved in a struggle for power; the loser seeks revenge and a cycle of destruction begins. To avoid manipulation, be yourself from the start. "This is who I am; take me or leave me" is the message that will give your relationship stability.

LISTENING

Men, in general, are not brought up to be sensitive and nurturing. This is a broad-spectrum statement and is certainly not true of all men. (It's also true that there are many women who are not very sensitive and nurturing, and you may be one of them.) You must understand your mate and decide if this statement applies to him. Most men are raised to value competence, achievement, and success as their first motivation. Caring and affection, listening to others, and sensitivity to social and psychological situations are learned skills for most males. It seldom has been demanded of them at any stage of their lives. Don told me he had to learn it through therapy and his support system of males who dare to be true warriors, sensitive and strong.

As children, most boys are encouraged to be bold, brave, and brassy. In sports they're taught to win, to want to win, that winning is everything. These life attitudes guide the adult behavior of many males.

Males often carry a take-control, fix-it attitude everywhere they go: work, home, social gatherings, even in church. At home, in an intimate relationship, this take-charge attitude can get them into trouble. They offer advice when it's not requested; this is especially true in conversation with women. The comic Rob Becker says, "Problems need to be fixed. She has problems. I fix them. I'm cave man."

When you want to release the stress of the day by talking about all things great and small, your mate may have a need to fix all your problems, to protect you, to give you advice, to dominate the situation. He may not simply listen. If you just want a willing ear, tell him that's *all* you want.

Listening is a learned skill. It doesn't come naturally to most people and may be as hard for you as it is for your mate. Most of us want to inject our thoughts and opinions into a conversation. This offering advice or turning the conversation around to you is not listening. Listening needs to be active. Being quiet is not necessarily listening. The speaker wants emotional support, empathy. If he's quiet, you may accuse him of not paying attention. Yet he probably can repeat every word you've said. He's paying attention but only with his head, not with his heart. You feel alone, and distant. Tell him you want heart listening not just head listening. Jessie, Laura, and Brenda all agree that their husbands have this head-listening attitude. Now when these women talk about their problems from work, they say, "I just want you to listen. I'm not going to do anything about this."

You want him to ask questions when he doesn't understand the issues you raise. You don't want him to fix the problem. That's your job. You have the capability to fix the problem and don't need his help to do it. When one partner tries to suggest solutions, the other often feels threatened and thinks, Does he think I'm incapable of solving my own problem? In listening, it's best not to speak, except for questions of clarification, until the person is finished explaining the situation. Then the question proffered should be "What do you think you should do about it?" or some similar probe to allow the speaker to solve his or her own problem.

The following conversation between two soul mates, Elaine and Chuck, is an example of nonsupportive listening.

Elaine: I think Mac is gunning for the promotion I'm supposed to have. I thought I had it in the bag but today Lester said I was going to have to go through some more interviews with the executive committee. He mentioned both Mac and I will meet with the committee on Saturday. Mac is only with us six months. He hardly knows our system but he plays golf with Lester. I've been in line for this job for almost a year.

Chuck: I don't understand. Aren't there set criteria for the job? Didn't they say that the senior manager had to have two years of financial experience, budgeting, and all that? Mac doesn't have that.

Elaine: Right! (Beginning to lose control) Somehow they think he can learn it quickly. He had some limited financial management at his last job. They're changing the rules in the middle of the process. One more time we women get the shaft. The good old boys stick together. Chauvinists! That's all they are.

Chuck: Wait a minute, Elaine. There could be another reason that makes him a serious candidate.

Elaine: Yeah, the executive director is his neighbor.

Chuck: Has he any proven management skills that they think you don't have?

Elaine: (Raising her voice) How *can* he? He's only in the manager's job six months.

Chuck: Don't yell at me; I'm only trying to see why they would bring in another candidate at this late date. It just doesn't make sense.

By this point the conversation had deteriorated. Elaine had lost control when she answered Chuck's first question, which took the conversation in the direction *he* wanted it to go. He never listened to what she first tried to say about the job. He wanted to understand and fix the problem, which, of course, he never heard.

Elaine is frustrated because of the new information she got today and becomes more frustrated when Chuck takes control and doesn't give her a chance to vent the way she feels. His questions may be valuable but before he asks them, he needs to hear her out and empathize with her feelings. He could have said right at the start, "That's a bummer. I'm sorry to hear that. You don't deserve to go through this." Then let her go on talking. This is heart listening; emotional support is what Elaine wants. She needs simply to emote in a trusting environment. Later they can be more logical and problem-solve.

Male or female, we all want someone to hear us out. Heart listening deepens a relationship. You must practice heart listening with your mate, then you can tell him that heart listening is what you expect from him.

When both of you simply listen and give support without advice, your intimacy will grow. Listening to you is a right you should expect from him. It's also a right that he has to expect from you. It's crucial to the development of a relationship.

CRITICISM

During courtship and certainly marriage, both partners need to feel secure and safe. If either is highly critical of the other, communication and intimacy will come to a halt. The one who is being criticized, the victim, will feel very unsafe.

Criticism is meant to change someone's behavior. The victim hears it as an attack, no matter how it's couched. An attack intends to destroy. We don't feel safe when we perceive someone is trying to change us. You've heard the statement many times: "I'm only trying to be constructive." This is a contradiction in terms. Criticism is by its nature destructive. Only the *person who is criticized* can make it constructive. The critic cannot determine the value of criticism.

Even when we ask for criticism, we don't accept it very well. A simple statement such as "How do I look?" often means "I look great, don't I?" You may want him to tell you if you have a run in your panty hose but not if you can't do anything about it immediately. The panty hose model can be used for just about everything. If your mate asks you for negative information, give it only if you believe he wants to hear it so he can change, and then as gently and kindly as possible.

If the person you're dating is trying to change you or you're trying to change him, then it's best to move on. For most of us, we are who we are and not much is going to change unless we *want it* to change. Only we can change ourselves. Negative conversations about us will not change us just because we hear them. Remember, this applies to both you and your mate.

Often we're critical of others and particularly our mates because we don't accept imperfection in ourselves. We think we must be perfect. We're always working toward it so we expect the same of others; thus we cannot easily accept our foibles. Remember that we're human and, therefore, not perfect.

We don't always listen well or love well. We don't always say what we mean. We say things that we thought were perfectly clear that others hear differently from what we intended. I don't think there's such a thing as perfection among humans so we should not fool ourselves to aim for it. Why delude ourselves that we should be perfect and that others should be too?

When we accept the impossibility of perfection, we'll begin to see the foolishness of our expectations. The mate you find is your soul mate. He loves you. You believe he's good-looking. He thinks you're beautiful. He respects your talents. He touches you and sets you on fire. He makes you laugh. He isn't, however, perfect. He throws his socks on the floor. He leaves the toothpaste uncapped. The towels will not be folded in triplicate and he won't always listen well.

You'll have to weigh what you can accept. If your tolerance of his behavior makes you critical, then you should move on or you'll become a nag. Romance will dry up. You'll be living with a negative self, which is worse than living with a negative mate.

When either he or you become critical, it's a sign that destruction is in your path. If it's early in the relationship, the struggle to give up the relationship won't be so difficult. If it's well into the relationship and you're in love and feel you've developed a certain amount of intimacy, then you will want to try to work at eliminating the criticism. Open, uncritical discussion can help. An uncritical discussion means that each of you owns your own feelings. You don't blame him for your reactions. "I get angry when you don't seem to listen to me" is owning your anger. "You make me angry when you don't listen to me" is blaming him for your anger. If you blame him for your feelings, he feels helpless and frustrated. He can't do much about your feelings when he doesn't call when you expect him to, but he can call you when he says he will.

If you find yourself being a critical person because you expect perfection, you may want to read some books on owning your own feelings. (See p. 221 for suggested readings.) If reading and trying some suggestions doesn't work for you, you need to see a good counselor who can help you. Being critical is definitely a big barrier to a healthy relationship.

Autonomy, Interdependence, and Conflict

Autonomy, interdependence, and conflict characterize marriage. Each person first needs to retain his or her essence in the union. We must first like ourselves, then we must know and understand who we are.

The individuals in our couples valued their autonomy; no one gave up his or her essence. Instead they shared their essence with their partner. One of Paul's core values is independence. He wants it for himself and for Jessie. He doesn't want to lose who he is. This independence, however, interfered with his reason for marrying, to be a husband and a father. Playing his trombone and sailing are also part of who he is.

I think that there must be a respect for the other person as a completely independent individual with her own life to lead. The best relationship derives from circumstances in which people are free to make their own choices. I think that Jessie and I choose to be together because we want to be. We don't set standards for the other's behavior. We both recognize that we have responsibilities as a spouse and a parent. A relationship that has that foundation will succeed.

Often somebody goes into a relationship knowing there's a real problem but thinks it can be changed. If we went into the marriage like that, it wouldn't have gone anywhere.

I didn't understand the type of commitment required in a marriage for years after our marriage. I think that at least in a first marriage, none of us know what we're getting ourselves into, especially where children are involved. We've been there for each other and undertaken all our responsibilities. It's a lot of work but it's also a lot of pleasure.

Cindy and Cliff exercise autonomy by keeping separate checking accounts. Brenda and Johnny make sure they have their own time. Brenda, a politician, likes time with the community. Johnny wants time for his computers, music, and tapes. Stan and Laura respected each other's career autonomy, living on separate continents for almost three years. Aimée is much more a social butterfly. Don prefers the quiet of home and a few friends.

What about your autonomy and independence? What do you need to preserve your essence? We marry for different reasons. If we wanted to be totally autonomous, we would remain unmarried. We come together for companionship, for support, for sharing, for the union of our bodies, and for the development of our common interests. We "couple" so that our life will be full and we choose a partner who will be a complement to our interests.

Autonomy and interdependence have a built-in tension in a marriage. We want both our independence and togetherness and it can cause problems. It's our willingness to preserve both that keeps the marriage alive.

Cliff and Cindy's conflicts are over their individual concepts of spending and saving money and their individual responsibilities in building and caring for their home. They both work long hours at physically draining jobs. As Cindy says, "I think we have equality in our marriage but it's at different levels. I feel it's not equal when he doesn't contribute to the care of the house."

Laura and Stan tell us of conflict in their styles of pushing their autonomy. One pushes and the other pushes back.

In every relationship there's some conflict. I told him when we were first going out that I'm a hairpin like my mother. I tend to get so tightly wound that there's little room for straight thinking. I'm a pretty emotional person and he doesn't always understand that.

On the other hand, he has very definite opinions about things and can be stubborn; not necessarily off-the-wall opinions, just ones that I don't always agree with. Sometimes I just listen and think what I want to think. Other times we have a "discussion."

Brenda and Johnny struggled over money and spending enough time together. Jessie and Paul struggled over Paul's passions for music and sailing, which took him away from Jessie. Aimée and Don, although only married a year, struggled in their courtship over their different financial values. Aimée wanted to start a new career and had taken the first steps to make that change when Don, a real estate broker, found himself in the midst of a real estate downturn. How was Aimée to reach her goal under these circumstances?

These are major crises faced by each of our couples. How did they survive? Some went into therapy. Others developed the skills they needed to make it work. All of them talked.

Silence is rarely golden. Often it's yellow, the color of cowardice. We often don't have the courage to confront what bothers either or both of us. Silence in conflict is valuable when it allows us to cool down. Used as a cover-up, to punish our partner with coldness, or to avoid the uncomfortable, it exacerbates the conflict and is a tool of destruction.

The couples wanted to make their marriages work. Brenda said, "The thought of divorcing Johnny was never in my mind. It was never an option." Because their initial relations were built on a foundation of friendship and respect, these couples' attitudes were open and direct. Cindy recounts a major blowup when Cliff went away and later returned eager to preserve what he had—a love, a friend, and a home of which he was proud:

> We hadn't been in our new condo very long when I went out and spent some money on a couch and he was so upset that he ran away for a day. I cried a lot because he didn't want me to get a larger condo and had talked me into a smaller one. So I went and spent a lot of money and decorated it beautifully.
>
> I was prepared to have him leave because I thought he couldn't accept my attitude about spending. I knew he had

been uncomfortable about that kind of thing. This was the last straw for him because I went all out and splurged. I began to think that I'd keep the condo until my next job transfer. I had already planned what I'd do when I got transferred.

When he returned he said to me, "I've spent the last twenty-four hours down at the lake thinking about my reaction. At first I felt you were punishing me for insisting on a smaller condo. I now know you only want to make our home beautiful and comfortable. I'll make a commitment to you that I'll never talk about that again and I'll never behave this way again about that kind of thing." I was so surprised! At that point I knew we got over that major hump. It released a lot of tension between us. There was a new sense of peace around the house. Now and then he has some fears of my overspending but he's stayed committed to what he promised.

All couples argue; some even have screaming matches. Robert and I have had screaming arguments, in the middle of which neither of us can remember what the argument was about or who said what to whom. Some say words they don't mean, like Brenda:

My brother had been a real jerk and I wrote him a rather nasty letter. When I was finished I showed it to Johnny. Halfway through, he said, pointing to a particularly sharp phrase, "Well, this is a little strong, and I think you should take this out." I smashed the letter on the table and I said to him, "I hope you die." I sat downstairs for two hours steaming, going over it again. Then I was able to tell him he was right and I revised the letter. I've never said "I hope you die" again.

He helps me see myself as other people see me, something I've never been able to do. He'd say, "Well, you need to know how people see you, because that could be harmful." He's my chief adviser. If my running for office hadn't been something he wanted me to do, then I'd never have done it. Instead, he said, "When you have gifts, you have to give them back."

All have confrontations. Cliff admits to not confronting as often as he should.

Why in all of these situations are these couples happy and fulfilled in their marriages? They've learned how to resolve conflict. Each and every one said they don't hold a grudge. Their attitude is, as Laura put it, "Life is too short to worry about the small stuff." Cindy says that she finds it hard to live with that "cold feeling of unhappiness that develops in an argument. I love the closeness that we have, the warmth, the hugs, and the laughter. I want that and I can't have it when I'm angry with Cliff. So I get over it quickly."

Marriages have built-in conflicts. Accept that there is tension in a healthy marriage. Both autonomy and interdependence are important but they conflict with each other. Conflict is uncomfortable. It makes some of us warriors and some of us willows. We must be willing to swallow our pride. We must accept that there doesn't have to be blame or guilt after conflict. We need to recognize that apologies aren't a necessary part of love. They may help to smooth hurt feelings but are we demanding an apology because our pride is hurt? If your potential mate wants to apologize, then great, accept it. But if he doesn't, then don't waste precious time in anger.

Humility without humiliation marks a marriage born in friendship and love. We don't need our lover, our friend, to be humiliated before we forgive. Certainly all apologies are not humiliating, but so often in the heat of anger and hurt feelings we feel we "deserve" an apology. That's what creates humiliation.

The warmth of open arms, laughter, melting eyes, and good smooching will be much more satisfying. When you're ready to be fulfilled in a marriage, to have this warmth and fire in your life, you'll be ready to give up your need to blame, to punish by cold silence, and to hold on to past anger. We should treat our soul mate like our best friend. How would you discuss differences with your best friend? How do you stay best friends?

Trust! Believe! Your marriage can be like your courtship when your spouse remains your best friend.

For the last twenty years many men have been focusing on being more sensitive to others, paying more attention to their own thoughts and feelings, and sharing their most personal feelings and self-judgments. More and more men are looking for closer relations with not only their spouse but also with their children and male friends. The good news is their numbers are growing.

If your needs for intimacy are high, you'll expect your spouse to be your close friend and emotional support. It's highly unlikely that anyone can be all things to one person. One can expect, however, that one's spouse, one's closest friend, will be willing to share intimate secrets. You must have some assurance during courtship that he has that capability. If he doesn't, be willing to move on. He's not your soul mate.

At all costs, this intimacy should be determined before you

make love through sexual intercourse. Sex for most males is a form of intimacy but not very bonding. For women it's very bonding. We're disappointed when the intimacy doesn't follow. We will discuss more about sex, intimacy, and commitment in Step Eleven.

In the next chapter we will look at falling and being in love. How important is it? Read on and you will see.

STEP TEN: FALL IN LOVE, BE IN LOVE

Falling in Love

Following *The Marriage Plan* takes courage. Falling in love takes courage. Are you willing to take the risk? Think of the state of nonlove. This is not necessarily the single state, but any station in life where love is not present. What characterizes it? It's isolation, separation, loneliness, unhappiness, disdain, self-doubt, not belonging to anyone, fear, doubt, unfulfillment, rejection, disconnection, frustration, and anger. This is not a pretty picture. Love is the opposite of this scene. Love is joy, humor, fun, play, compatibility, friendship, happiness, togetherness, companionship, warmth, building something together, making love together, delight, pleasure, intimacy, passion, craziness, belonging, peace, patience, harmony, beauty, affection. Most of us do not find ourselves in either scenario completely but we do recognize the difference when love is in our lives and when it isn't. Not only do we want love, but also we need it because it is the foundation of all life.

Are you afraid of falling in love? Are you afraid of giving yourself to someone? Do you feel it'll make you vulnerable to more pain? Is the pain you have experienced in the past so deep that it keeps you from falling in love? When we allow ourselves to wallow in the state of nonlove, we are giving tremendous power to the past. Rather than moving on from the person who caused the pain or the rejection, we are allowing that person to run our lives from a place that no longer exists. Intellectually this simply does not make sense. But falling in love is not dominantly an intellectual experience. It is primarily an emotional, soul experience.

Give yourself the gift of courage, to be open to the man who comes into your life to love you. Open your heart. Look at your body, your dress, your hair, your posture. Are you giving a signal that you are closed to love or that you are open to it? Sometimes the signals we give are contrary to what we want. Accepting me as I am does not mean that I should revel in being a slob or look like I don't care about myself. No matter your size or shape, you can dress and care for your body as though you are valuable. You can carry yourself with assurance and self-confidence and you can attract your soul mate. You must open the door to your soul mate. If you are hiding behind the mask of "I don't careism," he will not find you. You want to be physically as well as intellectually and spiritually attractive. Have the courage to fall in love. Make it happen for you.

Falling in love precedes being in love. It's a divine gift in nature that allows us to experience the prelude to real love. It makes us ready to accept the gift of true love. Remember the feeling of falling in love. It is the blood rushing through the body. The eyes sparkle, the face takes on a shine, the walk is more exuberant, and the smile is from ear to ear, ever present. We feel swept away on a cloud. We could take off and fly. People look at us and remark, "Something good has happened to you. You look radiant." Yes, our bodies tell the story. We are excited. Our sexual organs are on alert and we feel great. It's often difficult to describe but we all know the feeling, no matter what our age, fifteen or fifty-five, we love it. Being in lust or in love is a marvelous feeling.

The cause of these feelings is that the love is returned. Our lover looks at us with that same smile, the same rushing blood, the same exuberance, and this carries us through to the point of getting to know one another in a variety of ways. It is this craziness, this head over heels stage that can get us into trouble if we forget our plan. We need to, and can, enjoy it because we made a plan and we know that the person fits our profile. He shares our core values. If we let this feeling take over our lives, we will end up in bed before it's time. Take it slow. Live in the moment. Allow yourself to bathe in these feelings. Indulge your body and your mind in the luxury of the best feelings in the world. Love falling in love!

Being in Love

We will take this divine gift of falling in love and use it to develop our love. Often couples who have been married many years say that as great as falling in love is, it is the ordinary, everyday shared experiences that allow that love to deepen and their satisfaction to grow. Developing the intimacy, friendship, trust, and respect discussed in the previous chapter feeds our souls. The main reason soul mate marriages last is because they are spiritual. The couples rely on not only their God-given strengths, but also the continuous growth that happens to their souls and their marriage through shared difficulties, and even tragedies, as well as the shared joys of their lives. They give to each other every day in the little elements of respect that they show, the daily listening, the support each feels from the other when they take on challenges. They don't just say "I trust you," they practice trust. When suspicions arise, as they will, the soul mate makes the leap to trust. These are spirit experiences and they are the meaning of life because their nurturing is love.

When I talk to couples, both in interviews and casual daily experiences, and I ask them why they value love, they tell me that it gives them a comfort zone that nothing else can. They know they are loved for who they are and they do not have to wonder or fret about what they do or say. It's a different kind of bliss from the "suspended in air" feeling of falling in love. It's that rare combination of intellectual, emotional, and spiritual love that transcends the day-to-day drone of work, play, politics, or worry. When they are away from each other, they feel half of them is missing. "I missed you" doesn't mean that I can't function well by myself, but rather that when you're here I can do everything so much better. The soul mate marriage of many years finds the couple sitting in the same room, reading or thinking without having the need to say anything. Just being together is enough.

Words of criticism will break the love bond at any stage of growth. We want to tend to our love and eliminate any behavior that lowers the other's self-esteem. Words of praise, concern, and honest feedback when delivered with care can work wonders for the soul. Doing little things, thoughtful acts that relieve stress from our mate, are very important to keep the love growing.

Cindy tells the story about her concern for Cliff, who, in his fifties, is still doing hard, physical labor. She watched his body become exhausted at the end of the day and wondered how long he could keep up this work and pace. In the past they had had massages together but they were sporadic. She decided to arrange for him to have a massage once a week. On off days she would massage his body and then prepare a lingering bath for him. This revived him enough to eat dinner and then go on to bed. While she was working on his body, they would not talk but Cliff could feel her love. It was only after he relaxed that they began to talk about their days. These massages seemed to give Cliff more energy for his work. He seemed to be less tired but he wasn't willing to give up this newfound luxury. They did space them out, however, so that they had time for other things.

Robert and I have worked together for twenty of our twenty-five years of marriage. Yet often we would say we didn't have enough time together. The reason was that we wanted soul time. Time to talk about our dreams, our joys, and our sorrows. Work time can take that away from a love relationship. When the relationship is forming, focus must be given to soul issues to form the foundation of building these dreams. When you are developing your relationship, be sure you take the time every day to talk to each other. Keeping in touch by sense or by voice feeds the relationship and allows you to get to commitment and marriage by your deadline. It will also increase and enhance your love throughout your lives together.

Often in my seminars, women confront me with stories of their relationships that have lasted months, and even years, during which the couple are together only once or twice a week and don't communicate in between. The women want more but don't do anything about it. Anyone (man or woman) who prolongs a relationship like this is not in love with a soul mate. Many good things may characterize their relationship. It's comfortable, it provides sex, and it provides an escort for entertainment. It's not true, deep love, and it isn't the material that tasks the soul and allows it to grow. Such a relationship is certainly not fulfilling to the storyteller. I persevere in the hope that people in these relationships will have the courage to end them and proceed straight to the plan for finding their soul mate.

Falling in love and being in love are both characterized by passion. The flow and rhythm of the heart beats with an intensity of feeling that magnifies everything each mate does. The first is dynamic, exciting, and full of lust and chemistry. It's hard to sustain such energy for long periods of time. But couples who are in love call up this passion when their lives need it. The fire does not die; it simply continues to burn at a lower level that enables it to give off warmth, satisfaction, and beauty.

When we fall in love, our bodies take up so much attention. The lovers see beauty they have not seen before and they are in awe and wonderment. In deep love, the bodily beauty is still admired but the inner self is so much more important. Often I hear from Robert, when I'm sitting quietly or after we've made love, "You're so beautiful." It's hard for some of us who have many years on our bodies to believe these words but they're what make the love bond grow stronger and the marriage last.

Falling in lust, having the chemistry to make a connection with someone else, is the beginning of the soul mate relationship but it's only the beginning. Being in love and developing that love assure the couple of a long-term exciting, satisfying, and fulfilling relationship.

In the next chapter we'll discuss why sex before commitment can delay your wedding date and waste precious time better used getting to know your soul mate.

STEP ELEVEN: DON'T HAVE SEX BEFORE COMMITMENT

Sex and Commitment

A sexual relationship that includes intercourse before we've developed a deep, intimate relationship with our soul mate and before we have commitment will delay the time it takes to accomplish our goal. Women and men look at sex differently. For most women the sexual relationship is bonding. Thoughts of belonging, affection, and connection take hold. For most men, a sexual relationship is first a physical experience. This is not to say that they don't feel close and intimate when having sex; but for them it is not necessarily a bond. Sex changes the relationship. The emotions, passion, and chemistry take over and our minds become fuzzy. In the beginning, it takes priority over all other issues in the relationship and can distract us from our goal and our plan. We forget the profile we have so carefully drawn up. Our core values escape from our memory. We are emotionally hooked and we are headed for great pain if this relationship does not work out. When we take the time to develop the relationship without sex, when we zero in on closeness through openness, through sharing and listening, we assure our chances of getting our souls hooked first. Then we're ready for sex. Delaying a physical sexual relationship until the commitment is made assures you of that commitment if he is your soul mate.

In their classic study, *American Couples: Money, Work, Sex,* Blumstein and Schwartz confirmed a major understanding of the differences between men and women in their behavior and attitude toward sex. Blumstein and Schwartz studied heterosexual, lesbian, and gay couples. They were able to clearly identify characteristics of males and females in their attitudes toward sex. Females, whether heterosexual or lesbian, weren't comfortable with casual sex. Sex to them was a bonding in affection. They wanted sex in a monogamous relationship and with commitment.

Males were more comfortable with serial sexual encounters. Casual sex was common for both heterosexual and homosexual males. Sex wasn't necessarily an expression of affection, love, or commitment. It could be, but most of the time, especially in serial relationships, it wasn't.

Women in any sexual encounters read a message of love, affection, and commitment because that's how they feel about their sexual partners. Heterosexual women project onto the male the same intentions. They're hurt when their male partner cannot commit to marriage.

Effectiveness of Abstinence

Before Commitment

Many people don't see that the sexual relationship interferes at all with the commitment. You'll find that three of our couples, Susan and Mark, Laura and Stan, and Jessie and Paul, did not consider delaying the sexual side of their relationship. They saw sex as a way to get to know one another better. Sexual attraction wasn't the primary captivation. Their major attraction was friendship. "Sex was good but not a big deal. We just did it," said Paul.

For us other four couples, physical attraction had a strong draw. For Don, sexual delay was important in order to sort out his vulnerabilities. For Aimée, Cindy, and me, it was important to be sure that our heads were on the goal, to get a commitment before hopping into bed. We did not want to be confused. Brenda needed to develop a trust of men, and of Johnny in particular, before she was willing to make love. Robert and Cliff saw it as a matter of love and respect to delay making love until their future wives were ready. Cliff says:

> We did not have sex before our commitment to get married because Cindy established that point early in the relationship. I thought about it, but I knew the ground rules. It wasn't a high priority for me because our relationship was more personal than that. We had spent so much time to-

gether one-on-one without sex that we got to understand each other.

Aimée and Don both felt it important to delay sex to keep their heads clear about other issues. They wanted to be sure that they got to know each other in-depth. Don had many great sexual encounters but he hadn't had a loving, fulfilling relationship until he met Aimée. He had to trust his instincts about what was truly important to him. He wanted both and believed he could have them if he gave himself the opportunity to develop intimacy before having sexual intercourse.

Abstinence from sex is the most effective way of stating that you're very serious about your plan. If you're clearly dedicated to your goal, you'll keep a clear head about getting a commitment from your mate. If you're wavering about the commitment, then just how serious are you about getting married?

Carol, a young woman friend, had developed a relationship with a "terrific guy." She thought he was committed to her. He had said he wanted to marry her but they had not set a date. She believed that their relationship was strong enough to have sex. She was wrong. They had sex and it was very dissatisfying for her. He had a sexual dysfunction and when she suggested that he have it medically treated, he seemed unwilling and offended. She couldn't play games with him about this. She was unfulfilled and she broke off the relationship. She had not given their relationship time to develop into deep intimacy so he could trust her enough when she made this suggestion. If they had given each other more time in the relationship before sex, they would have known each other well enough to understand such strong feelings. If he had talked about the sexual dysfunction before she experienced it, she would have been more sympathetic.

What happens to your sex life if the relationship doesn't develop into the commitment phase for some time? You may want to consider other sexual partners. Since there's no commitment, there's no reason for you to be concerned about fidelity or loyalty to someone who will not make this commitment. A former sexual partner may be more than willing if you are.

Some people have been offended by this suggestion. They believe it would be dishonest. Other people believe that having sex with another partner could be too high a risk of losing their potential mate. If you feel this way, don't do it. Find what you need. You're in control. You make the decision. Just remember that having sex with your potential life mate before you have a commitment is a very high risk.

Robert and I made our commitment to each other within two weeks. We spoke openly about our willingness to commit and the necessity for abstinence until we did. Some women, when it comes to having sex, seem to be more susceptible to being subservient for the sake of keeping their men. When we do this, we're prostituting ourselves. We're giving up our most important goals for sex.

You may not make the commitment as quickly as we did and sex may be a much more critical issue to you. The chemistry is right, the love is there, but the commitment isn't. It's a difficult decision to make to abstain but it's the turning point for decision making. The message needs to go something like this: "I love you and am very happy with our relationship but I don't want to make love until we make our commitment to each other." It's not a threat but a considered statement of how much you value the relationship and where you want it to go. This statement will separate the men from the boys and the women from the girls. It will advance the relationship to where it needs to be for you or it will propel him out the door.

By making this statement you won't waste time. If this offends your partner, if he calls you old-fashioned or accuses you of playing games with him, you must be direct and firm and persist: "I'm trying to be very direct and honest with you. I know myself, and as much as I'd love to make love with you, I value this relationship and I'd like us to make a commitment to marriage before we do this. I want to make love knowing you're my life partner." Be firm but loving. If he's right for you, it will happen and it will happen quickly.

What Happens If We've Already Done It?

Many women ask me this question. "I have this relationship and it is sexual, and he won't commit but I love him, what should I do?" I suppose at this stage in the book, you will know my answer. Do you want marriage or not? If it's not important to you, then continue in the relationship. If it is, then you have to talk to your partner. Why won't he commit? I usually get all the same answers that we discussed in the previous chapter on commitment. "He's afraid because he's had two bad marriages," or "He doesn't believe in marriage," or "We've never talked about it," which is the most common answer.

I know many couples who have lived together for years and never get to commitment. This is not simply because of the sexual relationship but rather because they haven't taken their needs to be husband and wife seriously. There are innumerable reasons for this. They've had one or two bad marriages. They doubt their own ability to be a long-term partner. They may have been taken by an ex-spouse financially and they don't want to give someone else the chance to repeat this infliction. They just may not be sure their partner has all they need in a life mate. Basically, they haven't decided that marriage is good for them or that they want to be married.

Being married is different from living together. Remember, there may be dedication but there is not full commitment of total giving. Something is missing and that is that final act of giving oneself entirely to the other with no reservations. It's easier to break a relationship of cohabitation than it is to get a divorce. Instinctively the couple living together knows this. The pain may be nearly the same but the legal consequences are much different.

Suppose you're living with a man who doesn't want to get married but you fear that if you tell him your feelings, he'll bolt. If so, you're not being true to yourself. Do you fear losing what you have more than you want to be fulfilled?

Why don't you test to see if he'll ever marry you? The step that makes the most sense is to tell him that you want to get married and when. And if he doesn't hear you after you repeat it, then it's time to take the next step. One of the sure tests is terminating sex with the understanding that you want to come to a commitment to get married. You must do this only if you're willing to take the consequences of such a drastic action. If your partner still doesn't want to get married, then are you willing to give up the relationship to find someone who does? Answer this question before you terminate sex, because you very well may be terminating your relationship. Be absolutely sure you know and can accept the consequences.

Many couples come to commitment after a sexual relationship. Many couples live together and then get married but it's often only after a long period of time. They delay acceptance of commitment in marriage because one or both have what they want in the status quo. Often it's fear of commitment that keeps them from marriage. They're never forced to face that fear. Only later do they realize that they've wasted too much time treading water and never swimming to life goals with their partner.

Practicing Safe Sex

In this age of AIDS and increase in sexual diseases, practicing safe sex is a high priority. Do you insist on the use of a condom with your partner?

At what point can you trust your partner so that a condom is not necessary? The experts tell us that two negative HIV tests taken six months apart are necessary. You can never be sure since you'll be having sex with all the partners with whom your mate has had sex and vice versa.

Many couples are not only fearful of requesting that their partners take HIV tests but that they use condoms. They fear their partners will be insulted. Discuss it early before you get hooked. Yes, you need to develop trust but this is one area where no one can be sure of the health of his past partners. Insist on it. If he values his life, he'll insist on you also having an HIV test. This is not only a matter of your survival but of your children's if you intend to give birth. Take your life, his life, and your commitment seriously: GET TESTED!

Sex and Affection

Sex is very important to a relationship. If it isn't active and satisfying, then it becomes the most critical issue around which all other issues evolve. If it's alive and rewarding, then it demands less of our psychic attention.

Annie, who at twenty-six had some fulfilling sexual experiences but not very intimate relationships, found "the love of her life." She insisted that they take the time to get to know each other before having intercourse. They did and they came to commitment, announcing their intention to get married to their families and setting a date. When they had sex for the first time, he was a "wham-bam, thank you, ma'am" kind of guy. Although she was disappointed, she attempted to help him understand what pleased her and eventually their sex life became more fulfilling. They cared enough for each other to get some counseling and today they're happily married with a very fulfilling sex life.

For many women, affection is a critical aspect of lovemaking. Many women mistakenly believe that their male partners don't need affection in the same way that women do. They also believe that their male partner confuses sex for affection. One needs to explore these differences in the courtship. It's easy to determine some differences of affection through conversation. Hugging, kissing, and holding tell us much about these differences.

Donna, another friend of mine, is married to a wonderful man who cares for her deeply. They've been married over twenty years and he still withholds affection. To him sex is affection. She loves him so much that she's stayed with him and tries to get her hugs through friends and family. I wonder if I could live with someone without my daily allotment of warmth, hugs, and kisses.

She does. She's not looked for it in an affair but recognizes that she does need the affection with the sex and is working hard to convince her husband how important it is to her.

One of the problems many women have in their sex life is that their partner doesn't take enough time in lovemaking. It's seldom a slow, languorous, exciting process. It often has to be quick. In the discussion of what some sex therapists call outercourse lovemaking, they recommend touching and feeling as a first step to getting a woman excited, to pleasing her, to making her feel truly wanted.

Other ways of expressing sexual affection without intercourse are warm, passionate embraces, long kisses, body massages, body hugs, and quiet side-by-side body holding. Love conversation, words of intimacy, touching, desire, and excitement can express a oneness that's very satisfying. Delaying sexual intercourse and exploring each other's bodies in other forms of lovemaking can set the tone for a very satisfying and fulfilling sexual relationship. You can suggest what pleases you without sexual intercourse.

I've met many men who also believe that affection is important to their love life. They love women to hug warmly, hold hands, touch their hair, face, and lips. They shy away from rigidity and coldness just as women do. Abstinence from sex before commitment with one's selected partner gives a couple some time to explore their affection needs. It will also allow the couple to determine their sexual compatibility.

Are we comfortable in each other's arms? Can we talk about sex without embarrassment and with candor? Does my partner show affection sufficiently to satisfy me? You'll raise these questions and hope that the answers are easy to understand. Suppose they're not. Let's say you're not satisfied with your partner's warmth and affection. He's not a fuzzy, feely, hugging person.

Talk to him. Tell him what you need. He may have some hang-ups about expressing affection. Perhaps you can break through this shell or wall he may have created.

You may want to find out if he had much affection growing up. On the other hand, you could be with someone who simply will never satisfy your needs for physical affection. If very little changes after you tell him what you need in a noncritical way, you'll want to decide whether you can live with little warmth and affection or whether you need to find someone else. Are you getting your twelve hugs a day? You need them. If you're not getting yours, will you dry up?

You Read It Here

When your goal is marriage you need to be clear about your partner's intentions. Sex with your partner before commitment is not a sign of affection, love, or commitment. Commitment language and behavior are signs of commitment. Sex can mess up the emotional partnership when we want to be clear about our goal with our soul mate. We're talking about very temporary abstinence until we're positive about his being the right one. We don't want to mislead him on who we are nor do we want to be misled. We may end up marrying someone who is not our soul mate.

Once you are sure that you have commitment, sex will be very important to your relationship. You will need to explore this most intimate of relationships with your partner. Look forward to it as one of the greatest experiences of your life.

In the next chapter we'll discuss getting to commitment. It's the penultimate step of *The Plan*. How and when we get there is important.

STEP TWELVE: GET COMMITMENT

Get to Commitment

So many people ask me, "What is commitment?" They don't seem to understand a word that appears to be simple. I believe that they know the answer, that commitment is a promise to be faithful, to be exclusive in the relationship with each other, that it involves a dedication of one's entire being to the relationship, and that there is an expressed intent to marry. I believe they ask the question because they see so little commitment in relationships. At times it is their own relationship with someone that they question. Is there such a thing as a partial commitment? "No," I say, "that's an oxymoron." "Can you have commitment without marriage?" You can have dedication, which may or may not be permanent, but I don't believe that you can have a commitment.

Have there been people totally dedicated to each other who have lived together for most of their adult lives and don't consider themselves married? The answer, of course, is yes, but I don't believe that they have commitment. Commitment to me is one step beyond dedication. It's not holding back anything of yourself. It's not being afraid of a legal or religious bond. Commitment manifests a spiritual bond of a very deep level. Both parties recognize that this relationship is something they are banking their entire lives on. When someone gives that kind of gift, they are going the whole way and *that* is what marriage is supposed to be. Granted there are many marriages that lack commitment but for you who wish a happy marriage, commitment will lead you there.

Many people fear giving the gift of commitment to another. It may be because they have suffered so when their previous marriage broke up. It may be because divorce is so common that it makes a commitment easy to break. Or it simply may be that they don't feel the need to give or accept the gift of self from the person they love. We, as a society, have denigrated the concept of commitment. As we enter the twenty-first century, a greater sense of the spiritual seems to have arisen and people are beginning to take personal commitment in marriage seriously. Does this mean that the divorce rate will decrease? We have no answer for that. What we need to be more concerned with is our own willingness to approach the commitment of marriage. Marriage is not just passion, romance, sex, and love. It extends beyond these to caring for one another, growing with one another, and being loyal to each other.

Is divorce a contradiction to commitment in marriage? Yes, it is. If there is commitment, growth, romance, caring, and consideration of the other, and if both pay attention to growing and learning, then the chances of divorce will certainly diminish.

Showing Commitment

I'm often asked, "What are the signs of commitment?" "How will I know if he is committed?" The chief sign of commitment is not only a marriage proposal and the setting of a date but also the public declaration of your intention to marry one another. This sign is often regarded as the engagement. It can be an engagement ring, a public announcement in the paper, a party for your friends and relatives, an announcement to your family. Of course the first sign of commitment is when you agree to get married. But that is not enough. It must be public to affirm for you and all those you interact with that you have given the commitment to one another.

Hesitancy to give the commitment should be examined carefully. What is the person afraid of giving, or receiving? The commitment should not be given or received until both are convinced that it's good for both of them. Cindy tells us her story of commitment with Cliff:

> It was two weeks before that call came from Cliff. I hadn't seen Jim, the man I was engaged to, but we talked every night even when I was traveling on business. Cliff and I went to dinner. He wanted to see me again and again. Finally I had to make a decision. Cliff was insisting, after the first week, that I return Jim's ring but he didn't offer anything in its place.

We spent eight hours on the telephone having this conversation.

"Cliff, do you know what commitment is?"

"Yes, I'm committed to building my business. I work hard every day."

"I think you know what I mean by commitment. You want me to give Jim his ring back and break my engagement but why should I want to do this?" I was determined not to spell it out for him. He had to make his commitment to me on his own. He knew what he had to do but he wasn't saying it. Finally he said:

"I'd like to marry you, Cindy. I don't want you to marry Jim."

"Are you asking me to marry you, Cliff?"

"Well, I can't do that. I'm still married. I never got a divorce even though we've been separated for two years."

"I know that. What do you think you need to do about that?"

"I need to get a divorce."

"How long will that take?"

"I'll find out. I'll call my lawyer in Alabama tomorrow. Will you break your engagement to Jim?"

"You need to do some things before we become engaged. You do them and then I'll make my decision."

Although we didn't have sex, I knew I could goose him or kiss him on the navel and he'd love it. I was falling in love with him and I wanted him. I couldn't see kissing Jim on the navel or pinching his butt. I knew what I had to do.

Jim was always a gentleman. He understood. I told

him I couldn't marry him, that there was another man that I wanted to see. I sent him his ring. I've never seen or heard from him again.

Cliff and I became engaged in two weeks. With his ring on my finger, making love was everything I knew it would be. If it wasn't and Cliff and I couldn't resolve our sexual incompatibility, I'd have broken our engagement.

We were married within five months from our first date and well within the year that I had set.

The Marriage Proposal

Several of the couples, Susan and Mark, Brenda and Johnny, and Jessie and Paul, committed themselves to each other by moving in together. None of them looked upon living together as a long-term arrangement. It was a *prelude* to marriage. For some of the couples the decision to live together was a more difficult decision than getting married. Once they made the decision to live together, marriage followed very quickly for all three couples. Many people who live together do so without a commitment to marry; for them it's a substitution for marriage, not a marriage agreement.

The way in which the couples arrived at a marriage agreement varies greatly. Neither Jessie nor Paul could remember an "event" that they would call a proposal. Robert proposed to me at a dinner with his two daughters present. Cindy and Cliff had a proposal and a ring. Stan asked Laura four or five times before he got her to agree.

Aimée and Don had the most romantic proposal.

He asked me out for dinner for Valentine's Day. When he came to the door, he said, "I bought roses for you and I put them in the garage to keep them cold and they froze."

On the way to dinner he began making comments. He finds it very hard to keep secrets. He's shy in many ways but he tells many more things about himself than I would. He had this big grin on his face all night. He admits that he's been thinking and contemplating this night for a couple of weeks. I had hinted over those past weeks that if something didn't happen soon, I was going to be gone. By the time we got to dinner, I almost knew what was going to happen that night but I wasn't about to let him know.

After dinner when we left the restaurant, the rain and wind had stopped. It felt warm and we walked down to the plaza. We entered this place behind the wall of a monument.

"Let's sit down here," he said as he got on his knees.

"You're everything I ever wanted in a woman. I love you very much and I want you to be my wife."

Even though I had some idea this was going to happen, I was very overwhelmed. At that moment, the clouds went away and the full moon came out. I had tears in my eyes. Right after that, the clouds came back and it started raining. This one little space in time was perfect.

There were many times when I questioned my decision to set this goal. Telling my women friends reinforced my determination. They didn't know whom I was going to marry. I didn't. The whole year was like living in a fantasy. If it can happen to me, it can happen to anyone.

Brenda and Johnny have the most humorous story.

We had been living together for two months and Johnny had a heart attack. I took him to the hospital and they asked me, "Who's his next of kin?" I thought, Is it his mother or his daughter? But his dirty underwear is in my basement. That's all I kept thinking about. It seemed that I didn't mean anything. On Christmas Eve he had another heart attack and I went through the same thing.

After Christmas we went back to his doctor. The office is crowded. His nurse, Karen, put her head through the window: "We're giving Johnny a blood test to get married so you might as well get yours too." Finally he said, "Let's set a wedding date. We're going to get married on Valentine's Day. That way we'll never forget our anniversary." That's the way I found out he wanted to get married.

Two recent stories came from people who had attended my seminar. The first is about Suzanne and Josh. Suzanne had two boys from a first marriage, David, age six, and Jason, age eight. She set her goal in March 1999 for March 2000. Within two weeks she had met Josh, who was a perfect match for her profile. They immediately fell in love and began to see each other whenever they could, which turned out to be on weekends since Josh was a traveling computer software expert. He would call every night and eventually they talked about getting married. For her birthday in May, Josh invited her to dinner. He also invited her sons and his own parents. When the dessert came, there was an engagement ring on her strawberry cheesecake, on top of the whipped cream topping. Josh got down on his knees and there in the restaurant asked her to marry him.

Jason interrupted the proposal. "Mommy, I don't think we know Josh well enough to marry him." These wise words from an eight-year-old startled everyone in the entire restaurant, all of whom were watching the process. Josh turned to Jason and said, "Well, Jason, what do you think we need to do to get to know each other better?" Jason had the answers. They would spend weekends together and it would be better if Josh got a job where he could spend more time with them. Suzanne took control and asked Jason if she could accept on the condition that Josh and the boys would carry out their agreement. The proposal was saved and the marriage took place four months later and Josh did seek a job that would keep him home most of the time.

A second proposal happened recently to which my husband and I were witnesses. Friends of ours invited us to join them to celebrate Nadine's birthday on Halloween. We were in costume and simply enjoying the evening when Carl presented her birthday gift and a few cards. When she got to the last card, there was a letter inside. She thought perhaps it was a gift certificate. Instead romantic Carl opened his heart to her in the letter and asked her to marry him. It was beautiful and tears flowed all around. Even the restaurant owner wanted to make sure that she said yes.

All these stories are truly signs of commitment. They are indicative that the love between the two people was so deep that they wanted to share the moment with those people who were important to them.

In the next chapter we discuss the last step, getting to the altar and reaching your final goal.

STEP THIRTEEN: GET MARRIED!

This Is It

You have been waiting for this day, the day that you accomplish your goal. You are married to your soul mate. It may have taken you eight weeks, or five months, or even the entire year, but you did it right. You have fallen in love with the right person, the complement to your soul. You are in ecstasy because you know this is for the rest of your life.

What is so great about being married to your soul mate? Why did you want it?

It is time to go back to your statement in Step One and reread "Why I Want to Get Married." You may have written that you want to belong, that you want a family, that you want to share your life with someone, that you want to be happy by belonging to someone who will support your dreams, your fantasies, your hopes, and your goals. Whatever your reasons, you are now headed toward fulfilling them.

Your marriage is for sharing your fondest dream and hopes. If you stop dreaming, you stop communication with your soul. Remember that this is a marriage of souls, of spirits. If you stop paying attention to those divine and inspired wants and desires of your soul, you will be unable to raise yourself to one more rung on the ladder of fulfillment. If you stifle your creativity, you'll be unable to grow. You have become very connected to your soul mate. You know his desires, hopes, and dreams and you are committing to support him in achieving these. You have a partnership now. You are a team that is very much in love. Although you are two independent souls, there's joy in knowing that you are not alone, that you have joined together to encourage, care for, love, and support each other. There'll be good times and bad, sickness and health, poverty and riches, sex and abstinence. Sometimes the good times will be as stressful as the bad but you'll allow the sacred grace of your commitment to each other to carry you through them all.

You will experience surrender and resurrendering to each other. Each time you do you will move your relationship to the spiritual dimension. Your soul waits for that surrender where selflessness takes over and your self begins to grow, your soul begins to expand. This seems like a contradiction. Your self will grow to its greater powers when you become selfless, when your ego needs take second position.

When our self grows, we become more creative and operate out of our spirit, our soul. Being in love is a soul experience. Being married to our soul mate can be a soul-fulfilling experience. Enjoy it!

Partnership

You are now partners in life. You have a spiritual and an emotional partnership. You'll listen to each other's desires. You'll support each other's feelings without judging them. You'll respect each other's needs. You'll be there when you are needed. The partnership assures that you'll face the world together as a team. When the world looks at you, they will see a couple. When your families look at you, they will see the other. When we marry, we marry into a family, no matter how great or pitiable they may be.

Your families will now count both of you in their circle. Hopefully they will learn to love you. Whether it be stepchildren, parents, aunts, uncles, cousins, or grandparents, they will be trying to know you better. Being accepted into a family also gives you responsibility. You'll be expected to work at the relationships. They'll be looking for warmth, care, cooperation, help, respect for their traditions, and more frequent communication.

Family often takes patience. We need not be subservient but general openness to their life patterns is a good rule. Both families will look to your partnership for the lead. If you demonstrate affection and care for each other, they will know that your marriage is a good thing and they'll generally support you. There are, of course, exceptions. But for the loving members of the family, your affection and love for each other and for them will only encourage their love for you.

Roles

In a partnership each person takes on a role according to his or her respective talents, likes, and skills. You have hopefully discussed what roles you will take on in the marriage before this wonderful day. You have formed a household. Chores need to be done. Structure needs to be set up so that these chores never take priority over your soul relationship. Roles usually include a maid, a cook, a housekeeper, an accountant, a garbage collector, a laundry person, a chauffeur, and maybe a mother and a father. How will you talk about these chores? What agreements have you made? What happens if someone does not hold up his or her end of the bargain? Are you open to renegotiate the roles? Undoubtedly circumstances, such as a new job, children, or a new schedule, will call for adjustment. You both will need to be open to changes in your life that will necessitate a change in roles.

STEREOTYPES

Often roles in marriage are based on stereotypes for men's and women's work. We buy into our parents' and grandparents' concepts of what the partners' roles should be. Their roles may have been built on the agricultural days of the country—today we are in the information age and roles have changed. Your families may have stereotypes about what you should do, how you should raise the children, and whether you should not only respect their family traditions but also follow them. If you are a two-career family they may intrude their opinions on what you should do. The partnership should make it clear that this is your life and you'll respect their lives if they respect yours. If you are of different religions or ethnic backgrounds, this may be even more difficult. The families may be more interested in your differences than they are in your love and togetherness. Again, remember, the partnership is what counts. Your love, affection, desires, goals, dreams, and values are what will run your lives, not those of others, especially other members of the family. Rejoice that you have a partner to support you.

The Celebration

You have worked these issues out before this day. You have planned this day very carefully. Today is the day for celebration. Whether it be a large wedding or a small, intimate one, it is yours. It's time to celebrate, to party, to ritualize your marriage so that your memories of marrying your soul mate will be forever a cause for celebration.

All goals when accomplished must be celebrated in ritual. It is important to let the world know that two people place value on their soul relationship and have achieved the most important and powerful goal of their lives. Rejoice! Congratulations! Best wishes!

When we reach this goal, we are not finished. Now begins the work of developing this relationship into one that is deeper and more fulfilling. Before you leave, I would like you to move on to Part Three, "Conclusion," and look at some final issues for achieving your happiness.

Part Three

CONCLUSION

WHAT ARE YOUR CONCLUSIONS?

Who Are You?

Who are you in your essence, in the depths of your soul? That's the you that you want to preserve and nurture, the you who seeks happiness and fulfillment, who is looking for her soul mate for life. This "you" doesn't go away just because it's part of a "we."

Preserving who we are means that we have to know and act on those things we believe in, to understand those values that are central to our core. It means that no matter how much we cherish a relationship, we don't sacrifice our essence. We stand strong to maintain the integrity of who we are in the depths of our souls. If we're to grow as human beings, this knowledge of who we are and what we want will make a committed relationship last.

In trying to develop your soul mate relationship, it's important to be in control. To be in control is to set limits on what our mate might demand of us. If our mate demands of us something we believe that we should not compromise, then we damage ourselves if we give in to his demands. We must be sure of what we want to give and what we don't. On the other hand, setting limits based on fear or anxiety deprives us of opportunities to grow.

In setting goals, we set the limits in our marriage plan by determining how far we're willing to go with someone who doesn't fit our profile. We determine what is central to our core and what can be compromised. We set limits on how much we're willing to give and how much we're willing to take. We set limits on our time frame, on the profile we developed for our future mate, on receiving love and friendship, on developing intimacy, on support for our core values, and on whether we'll abstain from sex until commitment. These limits, when directly and clearly articulated, set the foundations for a healthy relationship.

These limits are not, however, the relationship itself. The love of two in marriage takes on its own character and, if nurtured, can lead us beyond the expectations that we set in our goals. We marry for adventure as well as love. It's not so much the adventure of our emotions as much as the adventure of our essence. To experience this adventure of exploring another, we must communicate who we are. That means we must be open and direct. This openness demands that we trust our mate not to abuse what we've shared. You've read about the excitement that our couples experienced in courtship. The intimacy they developed is what convinced them to marry. What made them stay married is the continuation of this intimacy.

The day that you visualized your partner after setting your goal, your desire, and your belief brought your imagined mate to reality. He's a real-life human being who needs nurturing as you do. Continue to use your desires, your beliefs, your visualization, your goal setting to assure your marriage is fulfilling. Do so, and you'll have what you set out to get.

It's all up to you. Do you believe in yourself? Do you believe in your right to find your soul mate? Do you believe that you control your own destiny? Do you believe in a power greater than you? If the answer to these four questions is yes, then it's time to begin. Perhaps you're not ready to set your goal. If you want to get married but lack the confidence to follow *The Marriage Plan,* there may be some personal baggage in your way. If so, then it's time to take a hard look at who you are and what you want out of life.

I want to assure you that once you set your goal, he'll come to you. But will you be ready to fall in love? Will you be ready to say, "This is my soul mate? I'll make him happy and he, me."

Setting the goal "I want to get married by such and such a date" says that you're ready to meet your soul mate. You're ready to pair with someone who will bring you joy, happiness, fun, laughter, excitement, sex, comfort, and peace. You are ready for the joy and ready to accept and work through the difficulties.

Millions of you are looking for mates. Some of you are searching for your first mate. Others are on your second or even third search. For all of you, single and searching, I've written this book.

All of us have relationships that make it difficult to make life decisions, and patterns of thinking and behaving that create blocks for us. We've been deeply hurt by past relationships and can't seem to forget the hurt or get past protecting our vulnerability. Life is complicated, and marriage does have difficulties. That's why I suggest that if you're not ready for *The Marriage Plan* you may not be ready for marriage; the time may be right to seek professional help.

Choosing a Professional Counselor

Never feel that it's degrading to seek help. Help is good. Who can help you? This helper can be a therapist, a psychiatrist, a counseling psychologist, or a relationship counselor. But picking a counselor is often risky and expensive. A diploma or certificate will not guarantee the effectiveness of the counselor's help. The chemistry needs to be right between the two of you. Choose someone by reputation and recommendations rather than through the yellow pages. Interview several candidates before choosing and don't leave your selection to chance.

Treat your selection as an investment, and make it worth your while. Ask your doctor for a recommendation. Ask some people who have had success with counseling or therapy. There may be a local association of relationship counselors that can help you choose the right professional for you. A group practice or a clinic may offer you choices of professionals and aid you in your selection of a counselor.

Check out everyone's credentials. Determine beforehand what kind of person would be effective with you. Do you want the counselor to be authoritative and directive? Or do you want someone to simply listen? Do you want one who will provide exercises to help you? Is the counselor certified and licensed in your state? Does he or she have the right academic background?

When you interview the professionals, tell them what you're interested in accomplishing. They'll then be able to quickly tell you if their expertise is what you're looking for and need. Ask what their philosophy of counseling is, what techniques they use, and what their client expectations are. Some will use tests; some will just want you to talk. The response you get will help you to determine if they have the right chemistry for you.

Finally, inquire about the counselor's fee and how long each session lasts. Most counselors will not be able to tell you exactly how long a period of time the counseling might take; it will depend on the progress you make. If you're determined to bring resolution to your confusion, or to learn how to become more intimate with a partner, then it may not require many sessions. On the other hand, if you have some serious problems to work on, it may take more time. Budget initially for ten sessions. As you progress, you'll learn if this is sufficient. Most counselors will be able to determine how much progress you're making. Don't cut yourself short and don't stay in the counseling relationship so long that you become dependent on your counselor. Once you choose your professional you'll need to develop trust in him or her.

The cost of professional help in money and time is always a consideration. Your medical insurance may cover some of the cost. Whether it does or not, carefully weigh what value professional help has for you. It can save you much heartache and the pain of fruitless relationships. It can give you the courage to control your own life. What you receive depends on what you put into it.

Will you work at resolving your issues? Will you be a cooperative client? If so, and you're convinced it will help, consider taking out a personal loan for ten sessions. Let the counselor know that your goal is to make great progress within the time you budgeted.

The gender of the counselor doesn't matter; what does is that you grow as a person under her or his guidance. Your goal should be to prepare yourself to be a happy, satisfied woman and a life-long partner, a soul mate, a lover, and a wife.

The Magic of Marriage

The magic and mystery of marriage lies not only in its extremes of joy and pain but also in the humdrum of everyday life. Surviving disagreements, and even battles and cruel words, is what helps us to grow. If we allow fear, anger, or selfishness to take root in our marriage for very long, love will disappear. The magic of marriage is in its openness, hard work, and words of respect, kindness, and honesty. It is in deep intimacy, tender love, frequent and innovative and exciting sex, honest and open conversation, and common interests, all spiced with romance and fun.

The magic of *The Marriage Plan* is in the words of your goal statement, in the dreams you dream, and in the vision you have of your mate in your meditation. The magic that you create will have the power to keep you together with your soul mate "as long as you both shall live."

Love and marriage is a mystery that has a spiritual dimension. Religions have always held marriage to be a sacred union. Our couples who have shared their love stories are not all religious but they all have a spiritual dimension to their lives. The special magnet that two souls create through their own giving is more than they could design by themselves. It has its own life and direction.

Because of love's mystery and magic *The Marriage Plan* works. Believing in yourself and in a power greater than you will attract a person somewhere out there who wants to join your spirit, who wants to be your soul mate. Are you ready?

Acknowledgments

Many people helped to make this book possible. Helen Moye, my dear soul friend, read many versions and motivated me not only to set my goal to get married but also to complete the book. Robert DeLaurenti, my soul mate for twenty-six years, read and assisted in editing, word processing, and solving computer glitches. Without the cooperation and inspiration of the couples who agreed to spend hours with me to share their lives, this book would not be possible. You know who you are and know that I will always be grateful.

To my first editor and mentor, Jerry Gross, you have been and are an enormous support. To my agent, Mark Ryan of New Brand Agency, and to my editor at Broadway Books, Cate Tynan, both of you have proved to me again and again that our literary future is safe in the hands of the talented and personable young. Thank you all for your wisdom and your kind and gentle suggestions.

I also wish to acknowledge the people who gave of their time and expertise in reading and rereading the manuscript: Vanda Carvalho, Mary Margaret Dickinson, Don McRee, Elysia Holt Ragusa, Brenda Jackson, Ruth Morgan, Nancy Riemer, and June Reinisch. Lastly, I would like to give special thanks to my daughter, Mary DeLaurenti, who had the courage to be direct in her feedback and to encourage me to continue in spite of it.

Interview Questions

The following questions were used to interview each of the six couples whose stories are told in the book. Each person was interviewed individually and his or her answers were recorded on tape.

1. Did you have a goal to get married?

2. Did you write down a date by which you would be married?

3. Did you set criteria for the kind of partner you wanted?

4. What were these criteria (religion, physical features, age, wealth, career, education, intelligence, and children)?

5. Did you write down these criteria?

6. What was your situation before you met your spouse? Were you single, married, dating, or divorced?

7. How did you meet?

8. What was it about your partner that attracted you?

9. How long was it into your relationship before you had "falling in love" feelings?

10. Please talk about the process of meeting and how your courtship began.

11. Did you date other people during the time you were dating your partner? For how long?

12. How long did you date before you decided to marry?

13. What were the circumstances that made you decide that this relationship was worth pursuing?

14. Did you have a commitment to get married before you set a date?

15. What signified your commitment? (Words, ring, gift, date to be married, any other ritual?)

16. What kind of fears or hopes did you have before you first discussed your commitment to get married?

17. Who discussed marriage first?

18. Did you have sex before you committed to get married? If not, did you have any discussions about having or not having sex before you committed to each other?

19. How did you determine his capacity to love?

20. What are your beliefs and philosophy and attitude about equality in a marriage?

21. Did you want to have children together?

22. Did either of you have children from a previous marriage?

23. If so, how did the children react to your getting married?

24. What are some of your characteristics that he/she must accept?

25. Did you have a discussion about finances before your marriage?

26. How have you worked your finances out during your marriage for individual purchases, checking accounts, joint contributions to the family, etc.?

27. What were your partner's needs for controlling money?

28. What were your needs for controlling money?

29. What were your partner's needs for "control" over other things?

30. How has your partner changed over the years? Has the change met your expectations?

31. How have you as an individual grown as a result of your relationship?

32. What advice would you give to people who want to set a goal to get married?

Bibliography

Allen, Patricia. *Getting to I Do*. New York: Avon Books, 1994.

Becker, Rob. *Defending the Caveman*. One-man play seen by author in Dallas at The Improv Corner, 1992.

Blumstein, Phillip, and Pepper Schwartz. *American Couples: Money, Work, Sex*. New York: William Morrow and Company, Inc., 1983.

Chopra, Deepak. *The Path of Love*. New York: Harmony Books, 1997.

————. *Seven Spiritual Laws of Success*. New York: Amber Allen Publishing, New World Library, 1994.

———. *The Way of the Wizard*. New York: Harmony Books, 1995.

Fein, Ellen, and Sherrie Schneider. *The Rules*. New York: Warner Books, 1995.

Gibran, Kahlil. *The Prophet*. New York: Alfred A. Knopf, 1923.

Gray, John. *Men Are from Mars, Women Are from Venus*. New York: HarperCollins Publishers, 1992.

Hill, Napoleon. *Think and Grow Rich,* rev. ed. New York: Fawcett Crest, 1960.

McGill, Michael E. *The McGill Report on Male Intimacy*. New York: Holt, Rinehart and Winston, 1985.

Morgan, Marlo. *Mutant Message Down Under*. New York: Harper-Collins Publishers, 1991.

Moore, Thomas. *Care of the Soul*. New York: HarperCollins Publishers, 1992.

———. *Soul Mates*. New York: HarperCollins Publishers, 1994.

———. *Soul of Sex*. New York: HarperCollins Publishers, 1999.

Schlessinger, Dr. Laura. *Ten Stupid Things Women Do to Mess Up Their Lives*. New York: HarperPerennial, 1995.

Tannen, Deborah. *You Just Don't Understand*. New York: Ballantine Books, 1994.

Recommended Readings

Chopra, Deepak. *The Path of Love*. New York: Harmony Books, 1997.

Gibbens, Kalyn. *Marrying Smart*. Rocklin, California: Prima Publishing, 1996.

Hendrix, Harville. *Keeping the Love You Find*. New York: Pocket Books, 1992.

Moore, Thomas. *Soul Mates*. New York: HarperCollins Publishers, 1994.

———. *Soul of Sex*. New York: HarperCollins Publishers, 1999.

Rosenberg, Helena Hacker. *How to Get Married After 35: A Game Plan for Love.* New York: HarperCollins Publishers, 1998.

Schlessinger, Dr. Laura. *Ten Stupid Things Women Do to Mess Up Their Lives.* New York: HarperPerennial, 1995.

Tannen, Deborah. *You Just Don't Understand.* New York: Ballantine Books, 1994.